FABRIC OF CHINESE SOCIETY

FABRIC OF CHINESE SOCIETY

A Study of the Social Life
of a Chinese County Seat

by

Morton H. Fried

1969

OCTAGON BOOKS

New York

Reprinted 1969
by special arrangement with Morton H. Fried

OCTAGON BOOKS
A Division of Farrar, Straus & Giroux, Inc.
19 Union Square West
New York, N. Y. 10003

Library of Congress Catalog Card Number: 76-75993

Printed in U.S.A. by
NOBLE OFFSET PRINTERS, INC.
NEW YORK 3, N. Y.

To my Mother and the
memory of my Father

foreword

To the average westerner China is so vast and exotic a nation that its nearly half billion people tend to be seen as a series of rather blurred stereotypes and not as actual people living in the context of their towns and communities. The old and trite saying that "all Chinamen look alike" to the western eye applies to cultural behavior as well as to physical appearance. Everyone knows, of course, that there are some differences between Chinese people of different economic and social classes. The general reader is aware that, although the nation is agrarian, there are wealthy landlords and there are peasants; and from Pearl Buck's *Good Earth* he understands the grim lot of the poor farmer and the value set on owning land. He is aware that China has great and ancient cities and that in these cities there are wealthy merchants, artisans, impoverished workers, beggars, and other classes who live very differently from one another. He has read of guilds of merchants and artisans, of secret societies, and of other associations. He knows that scholars are accorded very high esteem and given prominent places in the Chinese government. He has been informed that large, extended families form the web of Chinese society, and he has perhaps been led to conclude that kinship ties form the very basis of the governmental system itself.

These impressions represent a composite picture of China as a whole. They are based on scholarly and literary works which have sought to delineate what is typically Chinese, just as any people in trying to understand foreigners attempt to simplify the picture of them by reducing everything to the typical. The impressions are based on surveys of land tenure, land use, the family, the peasant class, the government, the secret societies, the religions, and other special subjects which usually treat China as a whole. Not that regional differences within the nation have been ignored. Differences between the north and south and between outlying provinces have of course been recorded. What the general reader on China has lacked, however, is accounts of how all the different facets of Chinese life—the economic, the social, the political, and the religious—interact within one another in the context of the local group where the people live. And, in lacking such accounts, he could not have known that the importance and the meaning of landlordism, tenantry, guilds, clans, family organization, associations and all other features vary considerably in different parts of China. Those most able scholars known as sinologists who have interpreted Chinese history and society for many years have painted the country in broad strokes, but they have not particularly interested themselves in how the principle features of the culture vary and interact with one another in the local communities. The other social scientists—the economists, the rural sociologists, the political scientists, and such—who have also concerned themselves with China in recent years have usually preferred extended studies of selected features than rather analyses of the interrelatedness of all features in a local setting.

A more intensive and microscopic examination of the local varieties of Chinese life has fallen largely to the anthropologist, whose traditional interest has been to investigate and record all aspects of life of small populations. Whereas he formerly devoted himself mostly to the study of the cultures of tribal societies, the anthropologist now also studies special segments or groups which comprise the greater society of modern nations. His method is usually to select a community and to live for an extended period among its people while he observes, participates in, and enquires about all aspects of their lives. If he is cautious in drawing conclusions he does not proclaim that his community is typical of the nation, that he has presented the total society in microcosm. Instead, he merely states that he has recorded a way of life representative of a limited region and that any insights his study may throw on the nature of the nation as a whole should be balanced by cultural studies of local groups in other regions.

Few cultural studies of Chinese communities have been made. Outstanding are those by Fei Hsiao-tung, Chang Chih-I, Martin Yang, and Francis L. K. Hsu. The total number of community studies cannot exceed a dozen. Even if one includes novels, the paucity of good material descriptive of the culture of the Chinese people is striking.

Morton Fried's study of the culture of Ch'uhsien is a highly significant and important contribution to the small list of community studies of China. Fried chose a community near Nanking on the Yangtze plain in a region where no such studies had been made. His understanding of the people of Ch'uhsien is based on an intimate and long contact. He lived in the community for nearly a year and a half. He spoke the language, and he not only observed and interviewed the people but he lived in a Chinese home and participated in local life.

Fried did not choose Ch'uhsien in the expectation of finding there the patterns of Chinese life in typical form. Ch'uhsien is of course Chinese in that it shares China's national institutions, but it also has certain distinctive patterns which differ somewhat from those found in other parts of the nation. The kinds of land ownership and land use, the nature of the family, the characteristics of the socio-economic classes and the interactions of these classes with one another do not wholly conform to the national stereotypes which have been created by previous literature on China. The point, however, is not whether Ch'uhsien gives a truer picture of Chinese types than other studies. It is simply that within the great cultural tradition of China as a whole there are many local variations, special combinations of features, and configurations all of which are Chinese but none of which can be said to be typical.

But Fried's analysis has a theoretical significance beyond that of adding to an understanding of the people of China. In Ch'uhsien, kinship relations are very important but they do not meet the needs of the manifold interactions between the different classes of landlords, merchants, artisans, peasants, and workers. Nor do guilds and other formal associations provide the necessary social and economic mechanisms. Fried found that there are also rather definite non-kin relations, such as *kan-ch'ing*, a special kind of

interpersonal understanding which serves to bridge the
gap between classes.

These observations bear on theoretical problems of great
interest. It has long been known that in primitive societies
kinship relations play a very important role in social
control, especially in small, local groups which lack any
formal civil government. The development of states and
nations is marked by the emergence of a governmental
superstructure which begins to supercede kinship relations
in many areas of behavior and which may even conflict
with such relations. There is certainly no better way to
analyze the functions and relative importance of civil and
kin controls than within the context of the community, as
Fried has done. While this problem has received compara-
tively little attention it is basic to any understanding of
nation formation. When more analyses like the present one
are available it will be possible to formulate general
hypotheses which are valid cross-culturally.

Unfortunately for western social science research in
China, the nation was swept by the Communists just at the
time when interest in the area had reached significant
proportions. Fried was one of the last of the western
scientists to work in the country. He left only when the
Communists were literally at the gates of Ch'ushien.

JULIAN H. STEWARD
University of Illinois

contents

Map of Area and 3 Charts

preface

The systems of consanguinity and affinity of a primitive people generally include most of their political relationships, thus the anthropologist working among primitive tribesmen has emphasized the study of kinship. Indeed, from the point of view of many aboriginal communities, society is populated with relatives. In the study of civil societies, however, complications have arisen which are unparalleled in the analysis of simple cultures. On the one hand, individuals in complex societies are involved in operating kinship units. On the other hand, they are drawn into widely ramified relationships which stem from the peculiar extended organization of their society. Both of these polar extremes have been studied in different parts of the world. What has not been treated, except in passing, are those relations which are intermediate between the two spheres, kin and civil, in any given civil society. This area of social interaction is labelled, for want of a better term, "extra-familial" or "non-kin," and consists of the social area which lies beyond the functional ties of kinship, either conjugal or affinal, yet which is not clearly included within the network of political or economic relations which are associated with the workings of the State.

Usual definitions of the state assume the existence of adequate facilities by which interpersonal relationships may be extended beyond the areas of kin interaction. Yet, as soon as one goes beyond this assumption and attempts, in a general way, to describe and analyze specific types of non-kin relationships, their functions and implications, an extraordinary lack of factual data is revealed. The present volume is intended to present a fairly detailed description and analysis of extra-familial associations in one large "community" of a major civil society.

Field work done in 1947-48 during a residence of almost a year and a half in Ch'u Hsien, Anhwei, east central China underlies the present work. The type of study made is known generically as a "community study." Ideally, such a study makes three emphases: ethnographic, historical, and comparative.[1] In the investigations of great complex societies, the community study method has a special value. It enables one to view, more or less in totality, a specific and functioning body of people which recognizes its own integration. The study of Ch'u Hsien, in particular, has additional points of advantage. It enables the analyst to view a political unit in Chinese society which is intermediate between the rural countryside and the urban centers of population. Ch'u Hsien, itself, includes rural and urban populations and is further stratified into

---

[1] Steward, 1950, p. 21ff.

social classes. The county seat also represents the functioning political unit through which the dictates of the national state are transmitted to the general populace. In almost every respect, Ch'u Hsien proved an ideal location in which to study non-kin relationships in the fabric of Chinese society.

The materials derived from field work are supplemented with data from the several previously published Chinese community studies and further information derived from general books and articles dealing with Chinese culture. Where possible, conclusions have been broadened, at times to Chinese society at large and, more occasionally, to remark on some general process in culture itself. While the approach has been, of necessity, largely non-historical, I have not refrained from using such historical material as was available and relevant. In addition, certain hypotheses, have been advanced which will eventually require historical validation.

II

Though the author bears sole responsibility for the accuracy of the data and the soundness of the conclusions drawn, he must acknowledge the source of much of his basic orientation in anthropology. Without the aid of Prof. Julian H. Steward, teacher, mentor, and friend, this book could not have been written. Dr. Steward not only discussed the concepts in the book but read and reread the several drafts and furnished detailed criticisms.

I would like to express my gratitude to the staff and personnel of the Social Science Research Council. The generous support of this body made possible the field work.

4

To the people of Ch'u Hsien goes my heart felt thanks. Despite the severest handicaps of war, inflation, and repression, they made my stay so happy and memorable that a bitter nostalgia arises at this writing. Mr. Mo-mo, and his family, my special friend Chen-ya, such helpful companions as Ken-chih, Yuen-k'ai and Mr. P., George and Marge Cherryhomes, and many others who cannot be named are all remembered with affection for their good wishes and eagerness to help.

Of the many others who contributed so generously of time, energy and ideas, I can single out only a few. Prof. Elman R. Service read the manuscript perhaps more times than the author and the final product has gained from his attentions. Profs. Arensberg, Goodrich, Kroeber, Strong, Wagley, and Wilbur furnished many helpful suggestions.

The present publication is made possible by a grant from the Columbia University Anthropology Publishing Assistance Gift. Special thanks are due Profs. William Duncan Strong and Charles Wagley for their support.

Finally, I thank my wife. Her patience and efforts, stimulation and criticism and her performance of so much of the arduous work, in China and at home, which underlies such a study, carried me through this task. This in many ways is Martha's book.

Morton H. Fried

Columbia University
July 4, 1952

chapter █

ch'uhsien

When the foreigner steps off the train at the Ch'u station, he finds himself about two *li* outside the East Gate of the city. First impressions are of numbers of small enterprises surrounding the railroad station and of great confusion and motion. Near the station is a waiting line of rickshas. A number of men detach themselves from their vehicles and offer themselves for hire. On the ride into the city through Great Eastern Street, one notes that the small enterprises near the station quickly give way to more substantial stores of varied types. Dimly glimpsed in the shop interiors are the clerks. They seem to swarm in the larger enterprises. Along the way, one passes a number of different handicraft industries. Men are seen working, nimble fingers weaving long strips of green bamboo into many kinds of containers, while young boys endlessly split the long bamboo poles into strips of proper size. A school teacher, clad in a uniform-like *Chung-san* suit with all sorts of identifying buttons pinned to his left breastpocket, receives the bows of his pupils as he walks down the street. He is one of the few persons who appears even slightly prosperous. Everyone else seems to be on roughly the same low economic level, evidenced by thinness of body, if not emaciation, and by poor and ragged clothing. The numerous beggars are clearly in the worst condition, but the differences, which at the first casual glance separate them from the working population, seem, to the untutored Western eye, to be quite superficial. It is only after a residence of some time that the confusions of the first impressions may be resolved into order and understanding.

LOCATION AND APPEARANCE

In romanized form, Ch'u Hsien is a common Chinese place name. In the original characters there is no such confusion; the Ch'u character has no meaning other than to designate this local area. The *hsien* character is of more general usage. It stands for 'county,' and, when combined with a place name, may mean either a county or a county seat. Thus, Ch'u Hsien means either the whole county that lies just inside the Anhwei provincial border across the Yangtze River from the former national capital at Nanking, or the seat of government of that county, an ancient walled town.

For the purposes of this book I will henceforth refer to the county seat as Ch'u and use the designation "Ch'uhsien" when referring to the entire county.

Ch'uhsien is in the Yangtse Plain. Rice, winter wheat, corn, cotton and sesame are its major crops. Soy beans, barley, yellow beans, kaoliang, buckwheat, and hemp are also grown. There are two important yields a year; the fall harvest is mainly of rice and corn, while wheat and beans ripen in the spring. The gardens, which are quite separate from the fields, produce throughout the year. However, the winter yields are small, and the townspeople as well as their rural neighbors, dry and salt a supply of vegetables for periods of winter scarcity. Pigs, chickens, ducks, and geese are kept in abundance within the town, and dogs are common. Water buffalo are only kept for market, and burros, while frequent in the countryside, are used in the town for turning grindstones.

Ch'uhsien is a Chinese county, one of about 1950 which comprised the Chinese national state at the time of the field study. It lies about thirty-five miles[1] north-northwest of Nanking. Ch'u has not had, in the past a consistent political orientation toward the outside. At times it has been linked with the northwest, as when it was connected with Huai-nan; at other times it was oriented to the southeast, as at the time it was connected to Yang-chou; the most consistent alignment, however, has been south toward the Yangtze River and toward the nearest great city, Nanking. This orientation has been induced in part by geographical features, since the river which flows through Ch'u enters the Yangtze just below Pukou, directly opposite Nanking. Today, Ch'u is most directly influenced by Nanking, despite the fact that the former national capital is in a different province. This orientation has been greatly strengthened, since the early years of the twentieth century, by a railroad, the Tsing-p'u, which runs between Pukou and Tientsin. Ch'u is the first express stop on the way north. At the present time, Pukou

---

[1] All distances are given in American miles unless otherwise stated. The Chinese mile, *li,* is approximately ⅓ of an American mile.

is linked to Nanking by steam ferries and small boats. Even in the older days, the river presented no barrier, but, on the contrary, was the easiest phase of the trip from Ch'u to Nanking.

The boundaries of Ch'uhsien have changed in the past, but the present limits have not been altered in a major way for almost half a century. Today, Ch'uhsien covers an area of approximately 600 square miles. It is roughly trapezoidal in shape, being narrower in the north than in the south. At its greatest dimensions it is about twenty miles from north to south and approximately thirty miles from east to west. The Tsing-p'u railroad runs in a gradual arc from the south-west to the north-west corner. Ch'u, the county seat, is on the railroad line about midway on the north-south axis but close to the eastern county border which adjoins Lai-an county.

Walls enclose the town in a roughly circular shape with gates at the four cardinal points. Only one of the four gates has a tower. Another gate still has remnants of an outer wall, a vestige of the past which is clearly illustrated on the old maps of Ch'u which may be found in the *Ch'u Chou Chih*. The town is not oriented about a single point or even a main street. The approximation of a main street, Central Street, is only one of several important streets. It is, however, the center of one of the two major commercial areas in Ch'u.

Most of the people of Ch'u live within the city walls, but families living within two *li* of the walls are counted as inhabitants of Ch'u. Most of these people are concentrated in four centers, one at each gate. The group at East Gate, which is nearest the railroad, is the largest. The street which runs from Central Street to the railroad is called Great Eastern Street and has two sections, one within and one outside the walls. Along Great Eastern Street are numerous grain shops, large stores, schools, and restaurants, in short, all of the services that may be found on Central Street except the banks, which prefer to locate behind the massive city walls. The importance of Great Eastern Street is enhanced by its proximity to the Ch'u river, up which, six months or more of the year, small boats come with goods. The "East Gate Outside" is also the site of the city's one mechanized industry, a wheat flour mill powered by steam. There are no notable conflicts between the town proper and East Gate Outside. The important merchants of the town generally have establishments in both locations; and the Guilds operate effectively in both locales.

Not far from the geographical center of Ch'u are two daily produce markets. East Gate Outside also has two daily produce markets, and each of the other gates has a small market. Each day, starting at about seven o'clock in the morning, gardeners, fishermen, and peddlers assemble with their merchandise. The markets are not the only places at which food may be bought. Grain, the basic food, is usually handled at well-established exchanges, each of which is privately owned and operated. Grains are not usually found in the general markets unless the price has risen so high that consumers can afford to buy only in the smallest amounts. On the way to market the vendors cry their wares, hoping to sell as much as they can in the shortest possible time. Most of the people of the market leave as soon as they have made their purchases or sold their goods. Thus, social activities in the market are largely confined to the processes of exchange. There is, however, intercourse among the various merchants and peddlers and some fraternization with customers. Particular places are associated with certain individuals, and there is some tendency for specific commodities to cluster at definite locales in the market. Many hawkers prefer to make their sales outside the market areas in order to avoid too keen competition of price and quality.

ANTIQUITY OF CH'U HSIEN

Ch'u is an ancient location. The Gazetteer of Ch'u, the *Ch'u Chou Chih,* refers vaguely to Ch'u as attached to various other areas in the past but gives little specific historical data until the Sung period (960-1278 AD).[2] It does mention, however, that Ch'u was a walled city during the T'ang dynasty (618-906 AD). The pinnacle of fame which was reached during the Sung dynasty is responsible for whatever renown attaches to Ch'uhsien today. Almost a thousand years ago a pavillion was built on Lang-ya Shan, the local "mountain." It was built for the famous poet and official, Ou-yang Hsiu. That gentleman became so intoxicated with the scenery that he wrote a poem in which he described himself as becoming drunk on the

---

[2] Cf. Playfair, 1879, p. 75:* "Ch'u . . . [an independent department] in the An-Lü-Ch'u-Ho circ., Anhui; Lat. 32°15', Long. 18°20'; [In the Spring and Autumn period, 722 BC-481 BC the town was at the] frontiers of [the kingdom of] Wu and . . . Ch'u; *Tsin,* in Chiu- chiang chün; *Han* in Huai-nan chün; *E. Tsin,* Nan-ch'iao . . . circ.; *Yüan,* (chou) in Yang-chou circ.; Ming, (chou) in Nan-ching province." (Chinese characters in original.)
* References give author's name and the year of publication. The bibliography appears at the end of the book and is arranged to facilitate location of sources.

view. Since that time the place has been known as the Old
Drunkard's Pavillion, *Tzui Wêng T'ing.*

Not quite a hundred years ago, the Taiping rebellion
brought a scourge of war to this area, the like of which
was not approached even during the Japanese invasion
and the recent civil war. As a result of the campaigns of
the Taiping rebellion, the population of Ch'uhsien was
so reduced that it might not be inaccurate to call Ch'uhsien a new society. Some local scholars estimate that by
the 1870's the population was reduced to one-third of its
pre-Taiping size. Much of the recovery since that time
may be traced to the return of *emigrés* and their subsequent increase. A large factor was the immigration into
Ch'uhsien of large numbers of people who came from the
outside. The places of origin of these folk point once
again to the lack of a consistent orientation of Ch'uhsien
toward the outside. They came from Shantung in the
north, Hopeh in the west, from the southern part of
Anhwei itself, and from Kiangsu to the east.

The Taiping Rebellion deeply affected the present social conformation of Ch'uhsien. Possibly it was an important factor in the development of the present pattern
of land tenure in this locality. Tenantry is widespread in
many areas of China. Some agrarian economists see the
most consistent development of tenantry in the southeastern and coastal sections of China, where the proximity
to great entrepots has been decisive. Such views stress
the importance of compradore investments in land:

Occupying ownership is least prevalent in the proximity of
great cities where urban capital flows into agriculture—in the
Canton delta 85 per cent of the farmers, and in the neighborhood of Shanghai 95 per cent, are said to be tenants—and

most general in the regions but little affected by modern economic developments.[3]

In Ch'uhsien, tenantry seems to derive much less from the expansion of investment in nearby cities than from reduction of the number of landowners during the Taiping Rebellion. The return of *emigrés* and the entrenchment of squatters does not seem to have greatly increased this number. Most of the indigenous landlords took up the holdings of relatives, who had perished, or of neighbors and friends, who had disappeared. The imbalance that followed, a relative surplus of land with a shortage of labor, opened the way for a large, if gradual, migration from land-hungry regions and facilitated the establishment of a large-scale system of tenantry.

POPULATION OF CH'U HSIEN

The present population of both Ch'u and Ch'uhsien is known only approximately. Various census attempts have been made, some ending in qualified success, others dying in the process and being forgotten. Since the Chinese citizen thinks of the census in terms of taxation and potential drafts of manpower, and since, as is shown below, there are adequate techniques for influencing and controlling the officials on all levels, this failure to obtain accurate population data is no surprise. The best estimate of the population of Ch'u, which is about 31,000, includes not only the people who live in the square mile which is surrounded by the city walls, but also the population which lives within a distance of two *li* of the wall.

---

[3] Tawney, 1932, p. 37; also compare Institute of Pacific Relations, 1939, p. 3.

The population of the county is less accurately known, but 150,000 is generally accepted by the county magistrate, the head of the local militia, the spokesman of the commercial guild, and various local scholars.

One of the few uniformities which bind these people without qualification is their racial homogeneity. All are Mongoloids, except two Catholic missionaries, who have lived in Ch'u for over ten years, and various transient Protestant missionaries and itinerant Russian and Gypsy pitchmen. Even the thousand-odd Moslems are physically indistinguishable from their infidel co-residents, at least without the benefit of protracted measurement.[4] Beyond this, dissimilarities appear and multiply. It is quite impossible to select a Ch'u man, label him as the average citizen, describe his life and then assert that the culture of Ch'u, much less Ch'uhsien, had been covered. It has already been seen that the number of economic specializations are great. Even among the people who are most closely connected to the land there are substantial differences of cultural detail between landowners and tenants. The Moslems are not the only religious group; there are Buddhists, Confucianists, Taoists, Christians, and combinations. Even language is not a homogeneous factor, since a number of dialects are present among the population. No kaleidoscope is capable of more diverse representation than this obscure Chinese county.

CHINESE SOCIAL CLASSES

It is not necessary, however, to despair of systematizing the wealth of apparently random data. There is one touch-

---

[4] It is not implied that the local population would prove homogeneous on detailed study. The range in physical type is wide but the most extreme differences are readily included under a generalized "Mongoloid" heading.

stone which, when applied, helps enormously in the task of creating a meaningful picture from such heterogeneity. The concept of class and class structure is not new to China. Long before the Chinese Communists appeared with their particularly class oriented messages, Chinese social theorists had understood that Chinese society is not structurally homogeneous. The classic Chinese class analysis deals with four major groups in the population; from top to bottom, the scholars, the farmers, the artisans and the merchants. There are also many special statuses, most of them regarded as *declassés* from the point of view of the scholars; these have included soldiers, actors, and ya-men runners among others. This classical concept is neither naive nor inapplicable, yet it is certainly inadequate for the analysis of contemporary Chinese social structure. Too many crucial statuses are not included and the order of grading is susceptible to deep criticism. The scholars of Ch'u were well aware of this and frequently complained to me about the reversal of social positions under the impact of new political and economic forces and the effect of long time inflation.

The anthropologist, Fei Hsiao-tung, made first-hand studies of class in several Chinese communities. Fei considers the peasantry and the gentry to be the two major classes in Chinese society.[5] Admittedly, such a scheme is even more simplified than the classical four-class theory. A major gain, however, is the clarification of one of the central facts and processes of Chinese society, the relationships between the landlord-officialdom and the peasantry.

For the present paper a modification of the classical

---

[5] Fei, 1946.

system and an understanding of Fei's contribution to the theory of Chinese classes is the best tool. In the pages that follow the social classes, as described, are largely descriptive, by which is meant that the emphasis is on the features, which, held in common by a given group, tend to give that group a distinct flavor and an independent character. Using such criteria, differences are stressed which in other contexts may be viewed as minor. Thus, for example, rich artisans, wealthy merchants, and prominent landlords differ greatly in the precise techniques and areas of wealth accumulation, but are very similar in their relationship to the basic productive facilities. Likewise, agricultural laborers and journeymen artisans do quite disparate types of work but are akin in the fact that they earn wages.

The separate groups resulting from the extensive division of labor in Ch'u are numerous. The most significant are the merchants, who vary from the great *laopan* controlling several shops and having influence in different kinds of business, to the *hsiao p'ao,* the small sidewalk merchant, whose entire stock may not be worth more than two or three United States dollars. There are also domestic servants, a large group made up of individuals of both sexes, who hire out by the season and who are generally recruited from farms or from poor laboring families with which the employer has some direct or indirect contact. The artisans are quite numerous and include blacksmiths, silversmiths, weavers, basket-makers, bean-curd makers, tailors, and a host of others. Service personnel is conspicuous, probably the most important being the men engaged in transportation, who use the wheelbarrow, ricksha, cart, or human back. There is also a large category of unskilled, unallied male laborers, who furnish a reserve for agricultural and horticultural work in season, as well as daily workers on transitory jobs. Such men may, for example, be employed to pull up the weight on a pile driver or to carry bricks and tile in the construction of a building. Lastly, there is the major group of gardeners.

The number of people who derive no income and fill no function other than that of landlord is small. Still smaller is the number of families whose income comes entirely from the ownership of land. Most of the small number of landlords, who are completely occupied in the administration of lands are engaged on behalf of a family or some social group. The other adult members of these groups are occupied in other activities, which are largely professional, commercial, or official and which are correlated with high status. The political bureaucracy is largely made up of members of landlord families and this has had great effect on the history of China. It has profound influence on the social organization of the town and particularly of the county seat which is the subject of our book. The correlation of office and land ownership is highest in the upper brackets of government service. On the hsien level, the landlord-bureaucrat group includes magistrates, secretaries, bureau (*k'ou*) heads, and the leaders of county districts. The correlation falls sharply with lower clerks, heads of population units (*pao* and *hu)*, and vanishes at the level of policemen, servants, and attendants. To describe a person in Ch'uhsien merely in terms of his economic specialization is inadequate. Other factors obtrude. There is a certain convergence of status and behavior within various specializations. There is also much overlapping in the performance of recognized roles within the society of Ch'uhsien. In the convergence of behavior we remark the tendency for all individuals of wealth, whether that wealth be obtained from land rental, commercial exchange, or the control of handicraft industry, to extend their periods of leisure and to desist from manual work. Wealthy merchants, successful artisans, and prominent landlords within their separate enterprises shift from the performance of jobs to managerial operations. Later, there is even retirement from active management and these persons turn to more remote advisory functions. Successful, wealthy individuals remove themselves from direct involvement in the affairs of their individual enterprises. They turn more and more to the general political structure, the local or national government. To be precise, one often sees prominent persons far more occupied with guild affairs than with personal business; with the operation of the local government rather than the polity of their families or extended kin units; or even with the operation of national rather than local politics.

The tendency for wealthy persons, of all types of specialization, to move into broader categories is accompanied by a certain leveling of status among the various specializations. Thus, successful landlords, merchants, artisans, and officials tend to associate socially on a basis of approximate equality. Wealthy landlords associate with wealthy merchants rather than with poor landlords; successful artisans prefer the company of wealthy merchants to that of indigent co-specialists. There is, however, an overall and generally recognized hierarchy of status which is reflected in the behavior and preferences of personal association of individuals. There is a recognized status of "gentleman' *(shih)*, held most generally by affluent landlords and rarely by even the most successful merchants or artisans. The leadership of the various guilds is often vested in a gentleman of the town; the leadership of the combined guilds is always so vested.

The overlapping of roles tends to confuse the picture of status and complicates class analysis. Landlords of decling fortune may enter commerce or handicraft. Merchants of increasing fortune often apply much of their surplus to the acquisition of land, thus becoming landlords. The elusive and changeable individual factor is of great importance. A man is known not only by what he is but also by what he was and what, in all likelihood, he will be in one year or ten or twenty. Likewise, to a certain extent, his background is important. To have descended of a literary family, one connected of old with the government, is a great social advantage. To be *nouveau riche* has certain drawbacks. Yet, neither of these eventualities is as important in Ch'uhsien as they are reported to be in Newburyport[6] or the "Deep South," U.S.A.[7]

Individuals in low statuses also tend to converge in areas which exceed the narrow confines of their respective specialties. Journeymen basketmakers, weavers, shoemakers, smiths, etc., also recognize their similarities to one another. The normal tendency in Ch'u, which was approved by the local government, was for the disputes of specific workers to be settled within their respective trades. This was institutionalized by having only one guild for a trade, this guild including both employers and workers. When recognition of convergence of interest led individuals to unite outside of the specialties the associations thereby formed were subject to intensive scrutiny and con-

---

[6]Warner, Meeker and Eels, 1949, p. 11.   [7]Ibid., p. 18.

trol by the government and by a united front of landlords and employers. When tenants of Ch'u united to stage a rent strike the movement was crushed; each participant was urged to bargain individually with his landlord.[8]

With these remarks on the complex nature of status phenomena in Ch'uhsien, we come to the six-fold occupational and social division which is employed in the pages which follow. The classes which are recognized, arranged in the order of grading current in Ch'uhsien in 1947-48, includes the following: officials, landlords, merchants, peasants, tenants, and workers.

Officials are those who are associated with responsible positions in the government, who, to some extent control their own activities, and who are recognized by the population at large, including individuals of all six of our classes, to occupy positions of power. These individuals may be incumbents or may have held office at some other time during their careers. They may be the sons or fathers, or to a less extent, the brothers of persons who are themselves recognized officials. Actual members of this class in Ch'uhsien include the magistrate, the father of the (then) Vice Minister of Education, a retired general, as well as other similar functionaries and their immediate families. Most of these people are also landlords. In this case the higher status is the one which gives them their class membership.

Landlords are those who derive their most significant portion of income from lands which they own but do not cultivate. Frequently, such individuals move into the class

---

8 Chen Ta gives an excellent picture of the clash of class interests, specialization interests, and neighborhood interests in industrial China. See Chen Ta, 1947, esp. pp. 187-191.

of officials. Some of them are descended from forebears who were officials. Within this class, however, political power is wielded not through official position but through manipulation of the rights of land ownership, manipulation of wealth, and by the use of favorable associations with officials. There are large numbers of owner-cultivators in Ch'uhsien, particularly in the western part of the county. These, by virtue of their labor on the land are not here included in the landlord class.[9] Likewise, there are many merchants and some prosperous artisans who have invested in land holdings which they do not operate. Their major incomes still derive from commerce or industry and I do not include them in the landlord class. This classification is not merely the abstraction of the present writer. The people of Ch'uhsien also recognize overlapping statuses and this recognition affects their behavior and the personal associations which they form.

Merchants and artisans, when examined in detail, tend to fall into two distinct groupings. However, there is a good deal of fusion between the two groups, particularly on the levels of greatest success and wealth. Rich merchants and rich artisans behave in much the same ways. They recognize affinities with each other and engage in extensive relationships with each other. Both are distinguished, as they grow more wealthy, by their progressive retreat from actual commercial or industrial functions. Merchants and artisans of wealth may invest in land. Though they are landlords in name, they do not enter the landlord class. In my analysis they do not do so largely because of the continuation of their contacts with com-

---

[9] Compare Fei, 1941; Fei and Chang, 1945, pp. 40-43.

merce and industry. In the minds of the populace they remain merchants or artisans despite their acquisition of land. This is the reverse of the situation in which a landlord, becoming an official, takes the higher status. Here, the lower status is maintained. Likewise, proceeding down the class 'ladder,' in each lower class the lower status tends to determine the class position of the individual.

Peasants are distinguished from tenants by their ownership of land. This is a category of nominal landlords which is not equivalent to the class of landlords because its members do not merely own land but work on it as well. It is difficult to draw a hard and fast line between peasants and tenants. Two major conditions preclude such a course. The first is the number of peasants, who, for various reasons, are impelled to extend the lands which they cultivate by the addition of rented fields. The second is the number of tenants, who, because of good fortune, are enabled to acquire additional land by outright purchase. The first alternative, though prevalent in certain areas of China[10] is apparently not pronounced in Ch'uhsien. In the second case, the tenant-peasant is considered part of the tenant class in keeping with the taking of class membership, in lower classes, from the lower status. Thus, though Ch'uhsien has some individuals who are wealthy tenants, these are unhesitatingly classified as tenants.[11]

---

[10] Buck finds large numbers of "part-owners" in almost all areas, but his statistics do not show whether these part-owners are moving upward or downward in wealth. Buck, 1937, vol. I, chapter II, table 22, pp. 57-59. Yang gives more sociological detail but omits statistics. Yang, 1945, pp. 132-34.

[11] The practical difficulties of classification are exemplified in the publication of the Chinese Communist government, *Decisions concerning the Differentiation of Class Status in the Countryside,* 1950.

Finally, the workers include both agricultural and hand-icraft employees. These individuals are generally proper-tiless and subsist on wages. The precise specializations in which they may be occupied are quite diversified.[12] There are various income levels within most of these specialties and a good deal of individual mobility. As the result of this mobility a given person may, at different points in his career, be a peasant, an apprentice-worker, an artisan or a merchant. Though this complicates the drawing of precise class lines and makes difficult the exact location of marginal individuals, it does not obviate the system of classes.

URBAN-RURAL FACTORS

The groups, which have been listed, are all capable, each to a different degree, of being split into an urban and rural component. This is least true of the category of officials. Even such officials as the heads of rural admin-istrative units *(hsiang-chang)* frequently reside or have their major contacts in the city. Merchants are also pri-marily urban, being located in the county seat or in the various market towns of the county. There are, however, certain types of peddlers and salesmen whose business it is to carry commerce into the hinterland. The rural-urban dichotomy is easiest to demonstrate in the instances of landlords, tenants, peasants and workers. Though the most important centers of landlord residence are the towns and cities, there are many landlords who continue to live on some section of their ancestral lands. For a number of reasons, including security and efficiency of management,

---

12 See Appendix I.

there is a tendency for outlying landlords to move into the town. This movement is incomplete, however, and it is possible to divide the landlords into rural and urban subgroups. Tenants, peasants, and laborers exist in both the rural and urban milieus. There are few important cultural differences between the town and country landlords. The farm operators who raise field crops, however, differ greatly from the town-based cultivators who specialize in truck gardening. These differing conditions affect all aspects of the respective subcultures; family structure, organization of the labor budget, standard of living, religious life, dependence on the market situation, are only a few of the areas of difference. Among the workers, there are important differences between individuals whose labor is confined to the fields and those whose time is spent on a loom or in a smithy.

The double axis which tends to divide and compartmentalize the society of Ch'uhsien, the class division and the rural-urban dichotomy, is of basic importance in the pages which follow. In the description of the various institutions, which are found in the larger society, it is never possible merely to describe a single example. Previous attempts to describe Chinese society on such a basis, for example, Lin Yutang's popular *My Country, My People,* succeed only in giving a picture of China as seen by a member of the urbanized gentry. It would be as valid to claim that such a novel as Lau Shaw's *Ricksha Boy,* which describes the vain struggle of a member of the Peiping lower class to find a secure place in the world, represented a rounded cultural picture of all classes. As various institutions are introduced in the present study they are displayed in a series of variations. The treatment is far from complete, but greater detail would obscure our central thesis.

It is incorrect to think of the county seat or town as other than an integral part of the county, but it is also an error to hold that towns are merely large villages. The basic wealth of Ch'uhsien comes from the production of the farmers, who constitute a majority of the population of the county. To this agricultural production may be added the labor of artisans who fashion usable commodities from raw materials. The bulk of the town population, however, relies on the exploitation of both categories of workers for its wealth. For example, the most immediate drains on the incomes of tenant farmers are rents paid to the landlords, interest paid to usurers, and taxes and assessments collected by the government. In Ch'uhsien there are two systems for assessing rent. There is a flat, standard amount of so many *tan* of rice and so many of wheat paid semi-annually; or a share arrangement, usually forty percent of the staple crops in season. Thus, at the outset, the peasant parts with a major share of the return from the land he has cultivated, giving the greatest single portion to his landlord. The merchant, who deals largely with landlords of farmers, is also indirectly dependent on the agricultural production of the *hsien*.

Guilds are negligible in village organization. It is only in the towns, where there is a concentration of specialists, that the guild fills a need. The farmers' guild, the one such organization that extends to rural villages in Ch'uhsien, is not the spontaneous creation of farmers but is a calculated structure imposed from the outside and staffed by officers who are semi-agents of the state.

Towns are distinguished from villages also in the institution of apprenticeship, a development which, in China, is largely independent of the guilds. In the villages, one learns by imitating and observing his parents, whether they are engaged in agriculture or in subsidiary handicrafts. In the town, young males are instructed in the techniques of some handicraft or commercial specialty, which entails a social relationship between master and apprentice that has no proper counterpart in the village.

A town is not only related to its agricultural hinterland, but it is also vitally connected to other towns and cities and through them with more remote entrepots and the world community. Some of these connections are clearly revealed in a consideration of how currency enters the town economy, an analysis that points up, once again, the ties of town to country. We have seen that a large portion of the grain produced is immediately earmarked for the landlord, an individual who frequently, and in Ch'uhsien generally, lives in town. The landlord separates from his rents the amounts he will have to pay out as taxes and the part he expects his family to consume. He then may sell his surplus in order to get cash to meet expenses for education, clothing, additional foods, and perhaps rent on his own house. The last, however, is generally paid in rice if the tenant is known to be a landlord.

The grain that is sold by the landlord will go to a local grain shop or to an outport grain store; in either case the rice is destined for the outside. The payment for the exported rice is always made in currency, just as commodities which are purchased from the outside are bought with cash and not bartered for.

Currency may also enter Ch'uhsien through payments for the services of various government employees and officials, from the Magistrate to the railroad laborer. In Ch'u, it is clear that the income the town derives from the government is far short of the amount it sends out of the community in taxes. Moreover, while the greatest part of the tax payment is in grain, the bulk of salary payments is made in currency.

Money is a commodity which leaves Ch'uhsien as well as enters it. A certain amount is drained off in the form of taxes, which the merchants pay in currency as opposed to landlords who pay in grain. Much of the outgoing cash, however, is expended by merchants, who buy consumer goods which are largely the products of Shanghai, Wusih, or of foreign countries. The importation of goods is an important matter in acculturation and culture change. The store system in Ch'u has special shops carrying outport items. One type of store, the *yang-tien* or "foreign" store sells items associated with the western countries, such as *yang-huo* (matches) and *yang-yu* (kerosene). Other shops called *kuang huo tien* sell items that originate in the two Kwang provinces of the Southeast.

A more complete description of Ch'uhsien is not possible in the present space. It is hoped that the present sketch provides a setting for the data presented below.

chapter **II**

the role of familial kinship

All human societies have some sort of structural unity which is organized around basic biological relationships. The nuclear family, which consists of parents and children, is part of all larger social structures which are based on kinship.[1] Several structural analyses of Chinese society point to the nuclear family as the basic social unit [2] and repudiate views which stress large and extended family entities.[3] Despite a common belief to the contrary, the nuclear family is a relatively small assemblage, though varying in size according to the area of China which is

---

[1] Murdock believes that the nuclear family is ". . . universal, distinct, and strongly functional . . . [while] Linton . . . [states] otherwise." Though Murdock understands that many societies see the nuclear family only as an element within larger family groupings, he has been taken to task by Opler. Cf. Opler, 1950, p. 78.

[2] Cf. Chang, 1939; Lang, 1945, p. 147; Francis L. K. Hsu, 1943.

[3] Kulp, 1925; Kulp, 1930; Biggerstaff, 1940; Tao and Leong, 1915.

under consideration and the socio-economic status of the persons involved.[4]

Certain functions are common to all nuclear families. All must have techniques for dealing with procreation, child rearing and education, the allocation of political and economic power within the unit, and the provision of an elementary locus of unity based on clearly defined rights, obligations, and specializations.

In Ch'uhsien there is not only a variation in the average size of the nuclear family depending on socio-economic status, but also interesting differences in functions and ways in which they are carried out. Even such basic and general functions as child care and feeding show patterned variations.

The family of tenant farmer 'A' may be compared with the family of wealthy merchant 'B'. Farmer 'A' has an annual income which is barely sufficient to meet his yearly subsistence needs. His children are nursed exclusively by the mother. They are trained by the father, mother, and older siblings.

At a considerable social distance from the tenant farmer 'A', is the merchant 'B', whose household includes several scores of persons wholly unrelated to his family. Mr. B's young children are nursed and cared for by professional servants. When they are older, they play extensively in groups which consist largely of unrelated children. Between the poor tenant farmers in the countryside and the wealthy burghers in Ch'u is a great gulf, but it is bridged by such intermediate types as the wealthy peasant, poor

---

[4]Lang, 1945, p. 147ff; Wu Hwa-pao, 1936, pp. 166-7; Wu Yuey-len, 1936, pp.625-27, Lee and Chin, 1929, pp. 8-10, p. 49.

merchant or artisan. With these qualifications in mind, we shall now examine the basic unit which we call the family.

THE CHIA AND THE HU

It is probably only in the poorest families, both in the countryside and in the town, that the household *(hu)* and the family *(chia)* are identical.[5] The family of a tenant, who was living outside the South Gate of Ch'u during 1947-48, represents this type. A resident of the outskirts of Ch'u since the end of the Japanese war in 1945, this man was able to rent only some poor and hilly land from the government. On this plot, which was extremely poor in ground-water, he grew wheat, corn and beans. These crops returned him a bare subsistence income after his rent was paid. When his son died, in the winter of 1947, he was plunged into debt to pay for the very modest funeral. He lived in a small two-room, pounded earth and thatch house built by himself on the skeleton of an older abandoned house. In these two rooms he lived with his wife and their surviving son, who was about sixteen years old. This nuclear family lived in relative isolation since the nearest neighbors were in a small farm village about ten minutes walk distant.

Almost at the other end of the scale was the family with which I lived and whom I shall call "Mo-mo." This family, diagrammed in Fig. 1 a, centered about twelve persons. It included a male head, his wife and children, and two nephews, one with his wife, the other with his wife and children. The nephews' mothers made occasional visits, staying for several weeks or even months. During these

---

5 Compare Chen Ta, 1946, p. 22.

visits, the women were counted as full-fledged members of the *chia*. In addition to these relatives, there also lived together, under the same roof, a large staff of clerks, bakers, cooks, laborers, apprentices, oil pressers, condiment makers, an accountant, female servants, wet nurses, and, for almost a year and a half, a foreign anthropologist. The related individuals, the entire staff as well as the foreigner and other visitors who stayed for any great length of time, all constituted the household *(hu)*.

The *hu*, however, does not always include all individuals who live under the same roof. During my period of residence, the quartering of troops in private homes was commonplace. The Mo-mos played host to several officers and their families, but these military people were never considered part of the *hu*. For one thing, the head of the household had no jurisdiction over them, nor did he have any responsibility for their activities. Also, the ties between the soldiers and the Mo-mos rarely were strong or affectionate. Though the soldiers were co-residents, they were not accepted as members of the *hu*.

The Mo-mos lived close to other families of the same name *(hsing)* and were actually closely related to them. Each of these families was, in its turn, part of a larger household. Much of the waking time of the young Mo-mo children was spent playing with kin, but, within the Mo-mo household there were, all things being equal, more opportunities for non-kin than kin contacts. Things, however, are rarely equal, and social relationships do not necessarily flow along simple lines of proximity. Thus, the age, status, employment, and even the temperament of the parties become crucial as selective factors in social contact and determinants of social distance.

The term *chia* or *chia-t'ing* usually includes most of the meaning of the English word "family," but it is capable of reflecting a wider range of social forms than is usually found in our own culture. For example, in Fig. 1b, one may discover a minimum of three *chia* and a maximum of eight *chia*. In Fig. 1a, it is possible, according to Chinese terminology, to regard all of the individuals represented as belonging to one *chia*. It may be said, with equal logic, that there are really three *chia* represented on the diagram. The difficulty, stated simply, is that the term *chia* does not discriminate between nuclear and extended families, whereas we must.

Occasionally there is an attempt to avoid the difficulty by describing the nuclear family in Chinese as the *hsiao chia-t'ing* or "little family." In Ch'u, this term is not found in common usage. Likewise, "big family" or *ta chia-t'ing* sometimes refers to the extended family, which is a common residence group made up of all the sons and their descendants. Again, this term is not common in Ch'u despite its simplicity. More common is the term "old seven branch (family)" *(lao ch'i fang)* a recognized ideal for extended families.[6] It is also possible to say "old three . . .", "old four . . ." or even "old five branch (family)."

The group composed of parents and children is always identified as a *chia*. It corresponds to a minimum definition of the family in Chinese society. Before defining the maximum limits of the *chia*, however, it is necessary to discuss the phenomenon of family splitting.

The Chinese extended family tends to become more brittle as the number of nuclear families which compose

---

6 Lang, 1945, pp. 13-15. Lang uses all of these terms.

it increases and as the financial circumstances which surround it deteriorate. An extended family, which includes a number of daughters-in-law, who have been diversely recruited, and which finds itself in either a narrowing or too slowly improving economic position, tends to fragment. It may resolve itself, either into a number of discrete nuclear families, each with a roughly equivalent portion of the total wealth, or into a new alignment of nuclear families, which make up two or more, new, but smaller, extended families. The latter eventuality is rare, at least in Ch'uhsien, since fragmentation, once begun, is likely to continue until the lowest common denominator of nuclear family membership is reached.

Division of an extended family in Ch'uhsien, except in rare instances, implies physical dispersement. A single house, with a single gate and many rooms, no longer suffices, but each unit now lives apart.[7] The situation in which ties of the extended family become materially weakened through physical separation is difficult to describe in general terms. China has long had a system whereby officials served in places remote from their own homes. Not only did such separation often fail to diminish family bonds, but often it had the opposite effect.[8] Membership in an extended family, however, frequently becomes weak and attenuated through separation and long absence. This is in contrast to membership in the nuclear family, since many such families take institutionalized steps to insure

---

[7] Compare the Min-chia in Yunnan whose family splitting is often expressed merely by moving to a new wing of the house. Fitzgerald, 1941, p. 87; Francis L. K. Hsu, 1948, p. 115.

[8] See Lattimore, 1950, pp. 50, 140, etc., for the extensive nepotism of the Hunanese and others in Sinkiang, etc.

the continued participation of absent members.[9] Though the people of Ch'u do not go to any great lengths to maintain the symbolic presence of absent family members, one is always considered a member of the family regardless of the distance or length in time of his separation.[10]

Daniel H. Kulp, whose study of 'Phenix' Village in Kwangtung is one of the first community studies in China,[11] was greatly troubled by the problem of defining and precisely locating the *chia*. Impressed by the importance of kin principles in the orientation of Chinese village society to the point of subtitling his work "The Sociology of Familism," Kulp was unwilling to classify all of the manifold functions of the *chia* under one heading. He found it necessary to define four major functions, each of which was associated with a special type of family. His divisions include the natural-family, which is based on sex and reproduction; the conventional-family, which is based on the unilinear extension of relationship through the male line; the religious-family, which is the unit which participates in ancestor worship; and the economic-family, which is "what is commonly referred to by the Chinese as the family." [12] Kulp admits that the above family types often coincide, but he is struck by the fact that the personnel of the various groups, though overlapping, is rarely identical. It is also implicit in Kulp's material that any of

---

[9] In Taitou, Shantung, places are set at ceremonial dinners for all the absent members of the nuclear family. Yang, 1945, p. 78.

[10] Cf. Lang, 1945, p. 14ff; Chen Ta, 1940, p. 118ff, especially Tables 12, 13 and 14; Lin, 1947, ˌpp. 122-41.

[11] An earlier work by Arthur H. Smith is sometimes thought of as the pioneer study. However, that work, though anticipating many later studies, was not based on the assumptions and methods of present day community analysis. Smith, 1899.

[12] Kulp, 1925, p. 142-48.

the four types of families may be composed of members who are distributed beyond the confines of one locality.

Kulp's categories do not apply too well in Ch'uhsien. The Chinese word *tsu,* frequently rendered into English as "clan," generally covers the ground which Kulp has included under the conventional-family.[13] The "religious-family" in Ch'uhsien hardly exists as a discrete entity. The worship of ancestors and the observance of calendrical festivals are relatively minor events in the lives of most families. The religious family was not the center of social control in Ch'uhsien. Recorded differences between Phenix and Ch'uhsien may reflect either changes which occurred during the time which elapsed between the studies or possible regional differences. The latter hypothesis gains support in the data of other observers, which show that the *tsu* system (clan) is much stronger in the south than in central or northern China. Ch'uhsien, lacking strongly unified *tsu,* which would facilitate the extention of kinship obligations and privileges, could not readily develop a religious ceremonial group, extended along kinship lines.

If the *tsu* and the religious-family are two aspects of the same social unit, then the phenomena which are labelled by Kulp as the natural- and the economic-family likewise reflect each other. A complication arises, however, in the tendency for a number of natural-families to unite and form a single economic family. This factor, which obviously produces families which are functionally comparable but descriptively unique, has also been studied by Olga Lang. She defines the term family:

---

13 Certain exceptions as in Hu, 1947, pp. 9-13, also pertain in Ch'uhsien.

". . . in accordance with the current Chinese concept of the family *(chia* or *chiat'ing)* which was also prevalent in imperial times and refers to the economic family, *i.e.,* a unit consisting of members related to each other by blood, marriage or adoption and having a common budget and common property. Both the persons staying together and those temporarily absent are included."[14]

In the matter of variations produced by the amalgamation of nuclear families in various patterns, Lang adds:

The composition of the family shows great variations. Three main types are distinguished: the conjugal, the stem and two forms of joint family.[15]

Two further definitions show great uniformity, the first is by Chen Ta, a demographer and sociologist:

[a family] denotes a group of persons living together as a unit who are related to one another by blood, marriage or adoption.[16]

This definition served the purposes of census investigation and was applied in southwest China during the wartime research there. Since in a survey of 3,170,555 persons the final weighted average number of persons per family was discovered to be 4.84,[17] the obvious conclusion is that the prevalence of the joint or extended family as the household unit in Chinese social structure has generally been overestimated.

---

[14] Lang, 1945, p. 13.
[15] Ibid., p. 14.
[16] Chen Ta, 1946, p. 22.
[17] Ibid., p. 23.

The second definition is that of Hu Hsien-chin, an anthropologist:

The *chia,* which includes parents, children, and grand-children with or without their immediate dependents, serves as an economic unit and for bringing up the young.[18]

Hu's definition reflects her interest in the processes of child rearing but stresses the economic interrelationships as the distinguishing feature.

Data collected on familial organization in Ch'uhsien correspond to each of these descriptive definitions in varying degrees. Allowances must also be made for major differences which accompany specializations associated with each discrete socio-economic class. Thus, the family of a small peasant or tenant farmer will invariably be small and not extended. Such extensions as occur on this level rarely exceed the addition of helpless or semi-dependent old people. A poor hut commonly shelters a nuclear family plus one or both paternal grandparents. This type of organization, however, is not as widespread as a romantic Western tradition about Chinese culture would have it. Among the poor, old people are considered a definite economic burden, and their presence may cause much friction within the nuclear family itself, particularly between husband and wife. Thus, in such families, it is usual to find the old people pursuing productive tasks almost to the days of their death. In one poor family outside Ch'u's South Gate, both parents of the household were blind and could do no productive field or household tasks. Instead, they worked every day hand plaiting baskets of bamboo. The son was not considered unfilial. On the contrary, he

---

[18] Hu, 1948, p. 9.

was praised because, among other things, he had managed, despite great financial difficulty, to buy a fairly good coffin for his father. The coffin, kept under straw outside the hut, was a source of great joy for the old man.

The nuclear family with only one or two extensions is also associated with certain government officials whose work leads to prolonged separation from their native places. It was particularly common among the office-holders in the Cattle Station, a unit in the Extension Service of the National Ministry of Forestry and Agriculture. Frequently, under normal conditions of employment, individual members or whole sections of the extended family are dispersed into separate areas. Some members of Ch'-uhsien extended families work in Nanking, Shanghai, Peiping, and other places. Similarly, there are in Ch'u a large number of individuals or family groups which are detached from extended families in other provinces.

At the Cattle Station there were three major patterns of residence. The most common was that of persons from distant areas who resided individually within the compound of buildings which housed the Station and which was located about seven *li* outside South Gate. The main building of the Cattle Station had been planned as a dormitory for single individuals, but there were several married couples in residence. These couples considered their locations at the Station merely temporary, and moved into Ch'u as soon as able. A post-war housing shortage made this somewhat difficult and expensive.

The second pattern involved nuclear families. Married couples, with or without children, dwelt either in one of the two housing units specifically set aside for them within the walls of the city of Ch'u, or took separate quarters for themselves. The mechanisms which led to residence in the government sponsored buildings, rather than in private dwellings, are largely external to the present study, involving consideration of local rental structures, space limitations, and the desire to avoid, where possible, the quartering of Nationalist troops.

The third and least common residential pattern was that enjoyed by several extended families which had migrated to Ch'uhsien as units when their major bread-winner had been assigned to the Cattle Station. This was the case with the director of the Station and one or two of its higher officials. There was also a fourth possibility; though this did not occur to my knowledge among the personnel of the Cattle Station, it appeared regularly among the military. I refer to the taking of secondary wives or concubines.

The higher officials of the Cattle Station usually participated little in the life of Ch'u. There were, however, many lesser individuals and families, whose lives mingled with those of a certain sector of the indigenous populace. The implications of these contacts is discussed below in connection with non-kin relationships.

The military, present in large numbers in Ch'uhsien during the period of the author's residence, displayed a large range of familial and non-familial patterns. Unlike the hierarchy at the Cattle Station, it did not include, at least to my knowledge, any migrations of whole or parts of extended families. Military persons accompanied by families almost invariably were officers. A large number of officers apparently had married while in the field, taking wives in addition to the spouse who remained at home. Much of the information gathered on this subject is, however, suspect, coming not from the military itself but largely from the writer's friends and associates who were part of the normal civilian population of Ch'u. The women associated with the soldiers were frequently pretty, wore gowns of many colors tailored in the Shanghai fashion, applied cosmetics liberally, had their hair waved and sometimes even wore high heels. It seemed obvious to many of my friends that they could not have been virtuous women. Furthermore, military couples were frequently childless and this was taken as *prima facie* evidence of recent and probably temporary connection. In Ch'u, when local girls were married to soldiers, the marriage ceremonies were often quite brief, and lacked most of the formal ritualistic procedures which were synonymous with marriage in the minds of local citizens. Thus, there was no attempt to worship the groom's ancestors, the bride arrived in a rickshaw rather than in a conventional sedan-chair, and the wedding feast was enjoyed not in a home but at a restaurant or hotel. Under such conditions the solid citizenry of Ch'u looked askance at the marriage.

RELATIONSHIPS IN NUCLEAR FAMILY

To return to the nature of the family and its significance in the social organization of Ch'uhsien, it will be well to summarize briefly those interpersonal relationships and those behavioral configurations which have their loci within the framework of the family. These relationships have already attracted much attention, and the present study makes no pretense of substantially qualifying findings presented recently by others.[19] The object of our

_____

[19] See, Lang, 1945; Levy, 1949.

summary is to clarify kin relationships before tackling the more difficult and less explored non-kin aspects of the society. This review of data, however, will also furnish an opportunity to compare the specific types of kin activity which operate in Ch'uhsien with the generalized constructs of that behavior which, in the literature, normally apply to the whole of Chinese society.

There are eight possible basic relationships in the nuclear family: that of the husband-wife, father-son, father-daughter, mother-son, mother-daughter, brother-brother, sister-sister, and brother-sister.

HUSBAND-WIFE

The relationship of husband and wife in Chinese culture has come in for more than its share of comment by westerners, who have been thrilled by the exotic quality of a marriage between two individuals who may never have seen each other before the ceremony. Conditions in Ch'uhsien in recent years, however, have materially altered the conventional picture. The influence of the western world with its relative freedom of marriage choice was quite strong among the young gentlemen who had returned to Ch'u after living in Shanghai or Chungking as well as among their friends, who, without having travelled as extensively, were equally anxious to be "modern". It should not be thought, however, that a revolutionary change was desired or in process. Instead, compromise procedures were being worked out by daring individuals. A man would decide to approach some girl he had seen or met, and he would secure the mediation of a trusted friend or relative for this purpose. Marriage was the stated goal.[20] At the other extreme, however, was a form of peasant marriage, which spread in Ch'uhsien owing to adverse economic conditions. This form of marriage, in which a young girl is adopted for service and eventual marriage into the household, was not new in Chinese culture,[21] nor could its growth be said to result from increasing popularity. The peasants themselves most frequently characterized it as a technique of convenience, dictated by the exigencies of their declining economic positions.

The relationship of husband and wife is of interest here for the degree to which it satisfies certain normal drives while excluding recourse to non-related individuals. Reproduction, the provision of a socially recognized and acceptable heir, is a crucial function of the husband-wife relationship. In Ch'uhsien, this was the soundest and most fundamental aspect of marriage. The legitimate heirs of a man were his issue through his wife. Should the wife be childless it was permissable for the man to add another female to the family in order to make reproduction more certain. Actually, concubinage was not very prevalent in Ch'uhsien. There are some men in the city who have concubines, and I was introduced to a few rural landlords, who had more than one woman. These extra women, however, were taken not because the wife was childless but, in the case of older men, generally because of the pleasure seeking of the male. One young man had shocked the community by returning after the Japanese war with a Japanese bride. He attempted to install his Japanese wife by the side of his Chinese wife but ran into such pressure

---

20 Compare Lang, 1945, pp. 123-25.
21 Vide: Levy, 1949, pp. 90-91; Fei, 1939, pp. 33-35, etc.

from his family that he relocated his second wife in Nanking and commuted between his interests in Ch'u and his love in the city. The merchant with whom I lived disapproved heartily of this arrangement, saying that his knowledge of the financial condition of the man lead him to believe that the arrangement would end in disaster. Although he tended to place the major blame on the shoulders of the young man, he thought that the family had acted in a silly fashion in not making the best of it.

If reproduction is confined to the family, the same is not so generally true of sexual satisfaction. A large number of the young men of my acquaintance, including gentlemen, young clerks and merchants, had experienced sexual intercourse before marriage. Some of them, though married, occasionally visited prostitutes when travelling to Nanking or Shanghai. Some, who had been away from Ch'u during the war, had been on warm terms with women while away from home. It is noteworthy that Ch'u itself, during my residence, had few prostitutes. Most of them were beggar women, who offered themselves to soldiers for small sums. With Nanking so close, it was customary for a man of means, who desired a woman, to go into the capital, where elaborate houses of pleasure could be found.[22] There was one man who had been a merry gentleman with a local reputation as a poet and smoker of opium. His nephew relates that upon the death of his wife, this man had been plunged into utter melancholy, which threatened to see him waste away. The father of my informant acted as go-between and went to Ch'uen-chiao, a nearby county seat, where he arranged for the

---

22 Cf. Chao Ch'eng-hsin, 1948, p. 127.

service of a professional prostitute. The melancholy man was taken to Ch'uen-chiao, where he lived with the girl for a short time. The affair was paid for by a coalition of friends and relatives, and a swift recovery was said to have been achieved.

Within the classical Chinese nuclear family, the relationship between the husband and wife does not usually include companionship, at least for the first several years of marriage.[23] A wide range of behavior was observed in Ch'uhsien. In most of the marriages known to the writer there was a community of interest, warmth, and in most cases an obvious and overt affection. Probably the most remote relationships between spouses were those in which the husband was a shop clerk. These men were separated from their homes by varying distances; some came from as far away as Chinkiang or Shanghai, others, however, were only about fifteen English miles from home. Regardless of the distance, only those clerks who actually lived within the walls of Ch'u were permitted to retire to their homes every night. The other clerks rarely were able to go home more than once a year, being given an annual vacation for the purpose and remaining at home for two or three weeks. None of the clerks known to me established new and separate residences in Ch'u. Such a course would have been foolhardy for several reasons, not the least of which was the need for the labor of the wife at home where she served not the husband but his parents. The expense of relocating her in Ch'u was considered wasteful.[24] The typical clerk in a store in Ch'u enjoys the companion-

---

[23] Vide: Levy, 1949, p. 175 ff; Pruitt, 1945.

[24] For an amusing fictional description of a similar problem in a different stratum of Chinese society, see Lau Shaw, 1949.

ship of his wife for only a brief fraction of the year. Indeed, except in unusual circumstances, he spends most of his time in contact with individuals to whom he is either distantly related or not at all. The various apprentices found in the numerous shops, though generally younger and unmarried, live like the clerks, as do a large proportion of the artisans, merchants and peddlers, who work in the city. Many of these men divide their time between a family farm in summer and a non-kin commercial situation in the winter.

The peasant or tenant farmer's wife has a strong functional role in the family's struggle for subsistence. In Ch'-uhsien she works at almost all the field tasks with the men, in addition to performing the bulk of the domestic work. The son grows accustomed to the sight of his mother performing heavy work from which she will be relieved only by illness, advanced pregnancy, old age, and death. The poor merchant's or artisan's wife, does not work so arduously, but her day is long. She helps her husband manage the shop, often acting as a clerk. In the case of the artisans, the wife frequently takes a hand in production, particularly at such handicrafts as basketmaking and weaving, normally male occupations in Ch'u. The rich merchant's wife, on the other hand, performs little or no productive role in the household economy. She directs the work of the female servants and makes the cloth shoes and quilts which the family requires. With Shanghai-made and foreign goods becoming more and more accessible, even these last two items are becoming rare and in the most of the wealthy merchant houses in Ch'u the women play Ma-Chiang and the click of tiles can be heard from morning until late in the night.

The gentry families in Ch'u do not, on the average, come up to the level of prosperity of the wealthy merchants. Wives and mothers in gentry homes are given more productive tasks than the wives and mothers of wealthy merchants. The work day of the gentry woman, however, is not to be compared with that of a peasant woman in intensity or in its physical demands. The typical Ch'u gentlewoman has one or two servants. She may also enjoy the household services of one or more daughters-in-law if her sons are old-fashioned. If the son is "modern," the daughters-in-law will assist on their own terms and the older woman will complain of their laziness. In addition to doing a good deal of the cooking, the mother helps in the cleaning and generally has little aid in tending her infant children. During her periods of leisure, which grow more frequent as her children mature, the gentry mother occasionally plays Ma-Chiang but spends most of her time making shoes, embroidering, and gossiping. Though her primary companions consist of affinal relatives, she is often in the company of friends who are unrelated to her.

Ch'uhsien has many widows who, if they are of the old-fashioned gentry, as most of this generation are still likely to be, still feel keenly that remarriage is distasteful and somewhat immoral. These attitudes are shown clearly in their attitudes toward, and comments about, women of their class who defy the traditional ban. Outside of the gentry, the attitudes show a definite and gradual shift as one descends the ladder of social ranking. The wives of rich merchants are almost as firm in their resistence to remarriage as are gentlewomen but the widows of poor husbands and artisans are not only willing to remarry, but sometimes quite eager. Their value as wives, however, is not high. Those with children are least desirable. The peasant woman, too, has difficulty but since both she and her children have a certain labor potential and since she does not usually demand an elaborate income, she may be desired as a wife. Despite differences in attitude, however, the plight of the widow is only infrequently alleviated by remarriage and in the absence of her husband she must also fill the paternal role in the rearing of her sons. Where the widow lives in some sort of an extended family, the role of disciplinarian of her children is often assumed by a paternal uncle or in the total absence of males of a suitable age, by the paternal grandmother. In the observations of the writer in Ch'u, substitutions for the normal pattern of male authority were frequently unsuccessful and produced male children who were quick to tantrums and disobediences. It is interesting that, as soon as possible, the oldest son will be entrusted with the discipline and control of his younger siblings, especially the males. This responsibility, thrust upon the young man, tends to aid in his own socialization. It also substitutes a person more compatible with the social norms of the patriarchal family in the place of the female.

FATHER-SON

The father-son relationship is of crucial importance but one finds once again a wide range of phenomena which can be reduced to order only by sorting the data according to the criterion of socio-economic class membership. Thus, within the peasant or tenant farmer family, the father-son relationship is a close one, involving bilateral dependence. The dominant figure in the relationship, however, varies with the age of the respective parties and when both are simultaneously adult and capable, conflict may prevail. The young son relies on his father for his education. The older man teaches the boy the techniques of farming, the civil and religious responsibilities of the male peasant, perhaps a few written characters, a knowledge of the lunar calendar and the meaning of the almanac. As a very young child a boy normally enjoys a warm relationship with his father, who often tells him stories, plays with him, and rides him on the burro, if there is one. These activities take place when the farm work has been done for the day or the season.

By the time the son reaches the age of eight or ten his relations with his father become more distant and formal. The boy is assigned regular tasks on the farm, and no longer plays together with his father. Perhaps the warmest contact between father and son during this period comes when the father watches his son at play with other boys and indicates his pleasure at the boy's growing strength and prowess by smiling broadly and making audible comments to a friend. During this period, however, the father becomes more and more the major disciplinarian. Although the writer never witnessed any physical punishment of a child under three or four years old,[25] worse than a mild shaking, he saw many older children, particularly males, being beaten, sometimes with a stick. With increased discipline, the father and son move apart, often never to meet again on any ground of true warmth. The behavior which characterizes this period of a male's development is of particular interest since it is reflected in the relationship between master and apprentice.

------

25 Ages are given in English terms.

A major facet of the father-son-relationship, which cannot be duplicated on the non-kin level, is inheritance. The son has two possibilities for his future. He may manage to carve out a place for himself by success in crafts, commerce, or even by entering upon an independent agricultural venture. In the huge population, however, relatively few individuals succeed by their own efforts.[26] It is far more likely that the son's opportunity will depend on his inheritance from his father. The optimum inheritance among persons in this class is a small amount of land free of debt. Such a legacy, however, is not very common in Ch'ushien, since it is an area of high tenancy.[27] For Ch'uhsien the more common inheritance of poor agriculturalists is the right to continue as tenant on a particular piece of land. This heritage is not as secure in Ch'uhsien as in certain other areas, which have a concept of two land levels, the topsoil and the subsoil, which gives a considerable degree of permanency to tenants.[28] In Ch'uhsien there is no customary fiction giving the tenant title to the land surface and the landlord rights to the subsoil. Various manipulations of the landlord, which are frequently beyond the tenant's control, may see a shift in families after the death

---

[26] Compare Fei, 1945, p. 277.

[27] Buck, 1937, vol. II, chap. II, Table 22, p. 58, lists areas adjacent to Ch'uhsien as high in tenancy, in fact, a study of Buck's material shows that the general region in which Ch'uhsien is located, is one in which tenancy is much more extensive than almost any other large area. The present writer's observations, though not statistically validated, are in agreement. The problem is capable of several explanations, one of which deals with the situation after the Taiping rebellion, as explained in Chapter II.

[28] Vide: Fei, 1939, pp. 184-185; Chen Han-seng, 1936, p. 52; Chinese Economic Journal, 1927, pp. 87-88.

of the original tenant.[29] Once again we note a normal familiar relationship which is conditioned by the crucial presence of a third and non-kin party.

A boy will often rely on his father's contacts to establish himself in a new situation. He may want to become an apprentice in order to extend the range of the family economy. He may eventually be forced to leave the land because there are too many prospective heirs to make continued subsistence possible. In any case, in such situations his first recourse is to his father who will use his *kan-ch'ing* on his son's behalf.

Earlier we mentioned the reciprocal nature of the father-son relationship. This reciprocity has perhaps been unduly stressed by Francis Hsu,[30] who considers it a benign influence on the behavior of the individuals concerned. In Ch'uhsien the reciprocity was often disturbed. It is true that no case was recorded in which the aged parent was made to drift away or was actually mistreated. Without question the old father would be supported by the son. However, the father was expected, wherever possible, to continue some productive labor, as in the case previously mentioned of the old and blind parents, who were given materials from which to weave baskets for sale. It is also usual to see old people in the countryside engaged in gathering straw for later use or sale as fuel.

Within the class of merchants, the father-son relationship differs from each of the points made above. During early childhood the relationship is not usually as close as among farm tenants. The father rarely plays with his infant

---

[29] An extreme case of dependence on the whim of the landlord may be found in the Chinese Economic Journal, 1927, pp. 570-76.
[30] Hsu, 1949, p. 780.

child though there is a continuous range from the smallest merchants who spent more time with their children, to the great merchants who spent most of their time involved with their businesses. In the house of the merchant with whom I lived it was rare to see the master (*laopan*) having fun with one of his children. When he did relax and play with a child, it was likely to be with a young daughter. At such times the entire personnel of the shop relaxed perceptibly, taking advantage of the *laopan's* obviously expansive mood. The master of this shop took great pleasure in observing the play of his two sons when they were engaged with their friends and cousins in such a game as "Fighting Cock" in which two youngsters paired off, each hopping on one foot and attempting to knock the other down. These play sessions were held almost nightly during the long summer evenings in the open space between the counters within the store. The young boys, most of whom were children of the various shopkeepers, had the run of the stores for play. The children of the *laopan* of the grocery store (*cha huo tien*) in which I lived also had relatively free access to the huge ceramic jars which held various kinds of sesame and sugar candies. One aspect of the free relationship between the father and his young sons was the frequency with which he gave them small sums of money with which they bought small sweets and other edibles from passing peddlers. It is notable that the father was less liberal in this regard than was the mother, the father often refusing the children and sometimes reprimanding them for a bad or ill-advised purchase. The father also showed his regard for his sons by asking them on occasion to join him at the table for meals. Ordinarily, the children ate with their mother while the father took meals with the officers of the shop, partners in business, or friends.

The education of a peasant or tenant farmer's son is largely confined to agricultural procedures, social responsibilities and affiliated matters. It is true that where specialization outside of farm routine is desired, the son may be sent off to a town or city where he works as an apprentice. There he is under the direction of a master who in most cases is not related to him or is only distant kin. It is the normal procedure for a boy of any commercial or artisan family whose investment and return in business is more than minimal, to be educated formally, though this education rarely continues beyond elementary school or a few grades of middle school. There is, under any of these circumstances, a large section of the child's life which is under the direction of non-related individuals. As we shall see, this sector is considerably larger for gentry children, a point of some importance since descriptions of gentry childhood predominate in the literature. Some examples are available in the various biographies and autobiographies which are rendered in English.[31]

The unity of the agricultural family has not been stressed but at many points is fairly obvious. The normal settlement pattern in rural China differs from the widespread American pattern of dispersed farm houses. Chinese agricultural settlements are usually represented as small villages of clustered houses in which a number of farmers reside together. These villages are composed in many instances, particularly in the south, of people of a

---

[31] See: Chiang, 1945; Hsieh, 1940. Pruitt, 1945, records the observations made in wealthy houses by a Chinese servant woman.

single patronymic.[32] Under such conditions the child grows up in an environment which is restricted in potential personal contacts. Despite the fact that villages are close together, that small peddlers *(hsiao p'ao)* frequent the countryside, and that occasional visits are made to town, it is clear that the country child of poor agricultural origin has little alternative but to turn to his family for social contacts. In Ch'uhsien this pattern is reinforced by the tendency for a large number of tenant farmers, particularly those within the protective radius of the city, to live in relatively isolated circumstances, a departure from the normal settlement pattern. None of the preceding conditions apply in the city, where within an area of about one square mile there is a population of not less than 30,000. Again the children of merchants live in large *hu* and are surrounded within the household by clerks, servants, apprentices and others.

In the matter of inheritance, the general pattern observed for poor agriculturalists holds very well for the merchant group. Just as at the death of a farmer, there is a sharing of the property.[33] In the agricultural situation, however, there seems to be greater fragmentation of the legacy, each son working his share more or less independently and with a minimum of combination. In the merchant situation there is somewhat more cohesion among the heirs, who often work the inherited enterprise as partners.

Compared with agriculturalists, the mutual dependence of fathers and sons in the merchant class differs in patterns

---

[32] Vide: Kulp, 1925; Fei, 1945, pp. 133-202, especially p. 158.

[33] Fei, 1939, pp. 66-67, discusses property division in agriculture before the death of the father. My data from Ch'uhsien do not cover this eventuality except for merchant and gentry families.

of life security but is similar in the matter of obligations
to the dead. In the economic realm, a well-placed merchant
is in command of a relatively extensive treasury. Even during the years 1947 and 1948, when the merchants were
railing against the inflation and bemoaning the general
reduction in purchasing power, the big merchants were
well lardered. Several of the old merchants in town all retired and including, among others, former cloth merchants,
tea merchants, druggists, and a man who specialized in
goods emanating from the southeastern provinces (*kuang
tien*), were members of a breakfast club and assembled
once every few days in a big restaurant for wine, dump-
lings, and gossip. These men would lend an occasional
hand at the store, checking the accounts, supervising the
cash, but mostly engaging only in idle conversation with
their sons, relatives, and old friends and customers. Old
men value family unity highly. The mere presence of such
a *lao wêng* is often enough to keep a family, which is
racked with internal tensions, together until his death, the
split taking place as soon thereafter as seems morally per-
missible.

When a parent dies, the son is charged with responsibility for the funerary rites, selection of a grave site, maintenance of the grave and periodic sacrifices at the ancestral
shrine. It should be added that though these observances
are, for the most part, carried out in all sincerity, they also
serve to place not only the family, but also the recognized
head of the family in his proper status position within the
community. In this fashion the ritual obligations function
not only as a medium for the continuation of the reciprocal
parent-child relationship, but also as a method of validat-
ing one's position among friends and neighbors.

The gentry, the landlords of Ch'uhsien who depend heavily on income returned from the leasing of their family lands, do not differ markedly from the wealthy merchants in father-son relationships. If anything, the education of the boy was even less in the hands of the gentleman; a much higher percentage of these children going through the more advanced grades of education. There was, particularly in the older days, a potential division of interest between the merchant father and his son, the father an experienced businessman, the son a possible scholar. This split was ameliorated only by the fact that in most instances the father would be anxious to see the scholastic success of his son, figuring on the high prestige such a success would bring, as well as the degree of protection from extortionate taxation it would afford the family. Divisions of interest were less likely in the gentry family. The traditional gentry pattern, though exclusive, was represented as the generalized social ideal, hence deviation was unrewarding. The tradition, however, did not always function to the best interest of the gentry family. Many families overtrained their heirs in literary and bureaucratic skills to the exclusion of even the most general agricultural knowledge. The tenant farmers, being hard pressed, took advantage of the landlord's ignorance of farm conditions to reduce their share-rents.

Should the son of a gentleman desire to enter upon a career other than gentleman landlord, his way might be prepared by his father, who would bring to bear as much pressure as possible on all of those contacts, based both on kinship and friendship, which he possessed. During the Japanese War, several of the young men of Ch'u, who went into the army, managed to get commissioned through the good offices of their fathers. After the war and during my residence, a young scholar from Ch'u managed to go to the United States, largely through the machinations of his father, who was an editor of a Nanking newspaper.[34]

FATHER-DAUGHTER:

The fragility of the relationship between father and daughter has been pointed out by Marion J. Levy,[35] who considers the relationship of only "slight institutional importance" and "temporary." Considering the relationship basically one of awe and respect on the part of the girl, with the father remote and aloof, Levy also discusses "non-institutionalized" variants of the relationship in which a warm affection grows between the father and his daughter.

In Ch'uhsien, the state of affairs noted by Levy is somewhat modified. While it is quite true that in many cases girls, who have passed puberty, have very little or no warm personal contact with their fathers, there are many exceptions. As infants, the girls are quite likely to be affectionately dandled and fondled by their fathers, much as an infant boy is treated. In wealthier classes, the clothing of the little girl, especially on festive occasions, is bright and relatively expensive. During the years of childhood, from three to ten or eleven, the father treats the girls with more indulgence than the boys, especially in richer households. It is felt that the boys should learn from their fathers, but the girls are disciplined primarily by their mothers or other females who are mother surrogates. In poor families, the older girls, nine to fourteen, are actively engaged in

---

[34] For a rather grim account of the manipulations in which a father may engage to benefit his son, the reader is again directed to the novel, *The Quest for Love of Lao Lee,* by Lao Shaw.   [35] Levy, 1949, pp. 179-81.

tending younger children, if there are any. In a farming situation, the youngest girls take daily care of the water buffalo; older girls are employed at regular tasks in the fields or gardens in addition to performing various household duties and such domestic tasks as shoe and blanket-making. The farm girls of ten years and older are frequently sent to market to sell garden produce and, when operating in this capacity, they come fully under the supervision of their fathers, mistakes leading to disciplinary action. Finally, many farm girls are sent into C'hu, or other towns and cities, where they are employed as servants, often in the homes of the landlords who lease lands to their families. This situation is not nearly as common as apprenticeship for the boys, but it removes farm girls from their homes and subjects then to non-kin contacts rather than relationships based on consanguinity.[36]

A focal point of the father-daughter relationship is the marriage of the girl. In this event both father and mother figure importantly. In many instances it is the mother rather than the father who guides the selection of a match-maker or go-between. Frequently it is she who has the greatest influence in selecting the groom. The father's role is often as a court of appeal, but his general influence in the marriage as the basic provider of status is of great significance in the eventual provision of a husband.[37]

In traditional Chinese procedure, the female once married passed out of the scope of her natal family except for

---

[36] In the biography of Ning Taitai we learn of one Chinese woman who escaped her husband by working in an official's house. Pruitt, 1945, p. 76.

[37] Status as a criterion in the selection of a mate figures on all social levels but is of maximum importance among the gentry. Cf. Fei, 1946, p. 5.

occasional visits which grow more rare with time. The bride who returned to her family with the intent of deserting her husband, received small comfort.[38] The woman was not included among the normal heirs unless the family was without male issue. In Ch'u, among the landed gentry and in the upper stratum of merchants, a change had already occurred. Daughters were included in the legacy. This new development, which was, and probably will continue to be, supported by legal sanction, had not yet been set into a mold of fixed behavior, but other changes of a parallel nature were developing. The contact between the married daughter and her father is being broadened.

The son-in-law often is involved in these contacts and in many gentry homes in Ch'u the son-in-law was not an infrequent guest. To the knowledge of the present writer, this aspect of the breakdown of a traditional value of the old Chinese family structure has not been reported elsewhere. It seems hardly likely that such a new form of behavior, so well geared to a new pattern of property descent, would fail to become institutionalized.

MOTHER-SON

As Lang[39] and Levy[40] have stated in generalization, and Yang has described for the village of Taitou in Southeastern Shantung,[41] the relationship between mother and son is affectionate. The mother, unless widowed, is a major disciplinarian only for the first few years of life. By the time the boy is about ten years old (in both Taitou and

---

[38] Pruitt, *op. cit.,* gives a picture of institutionalized visiting (p. 43) and of the lack of sympathy for permanent returns to the family (p. 32). [39] Lang, 1945, pp. 29-30.   [40] Levy, 1949, pp. 181-183.   [41] Yang, 1945, pp. 58-59.   [42] Ibid., p. 58

Ch'uhsien) the main source of home discipline is the father. As a small child, however, the boy receives most of his punishment from his mother or from her surrogates, the oldest sisters, or her agents, the child's older brothers. It is noteworthy that the right and obligation of older brothers to discipline their younger siblings, when the older brother is himself not older than twelve or fourteen years, is sanctioned by the mother, who personally observes the process, rather than by the father, who is normally distant from the proceedings. During those years which we call young manhood and which are more or less covered by the term *ch'ing nien* in Chinese, the mother is replaced by the father as the source of major disciplinary sanction. It is during this period that the mother cements her relationship with her son and may become his confidant to some limited extent. This position of confidant, however, is more usually held by a close friend. Yang reports that the mother-son contact at this period is strengthened as the mother casts about for a wife for her son.[42] The son discusses his hopes and desires and frequently has a sympathetic listener in his mother. In Ch'u, where new mating conventions have begun to penetrate, the patterns of marital allignment are already effecting changes in this particular complex of behavioral relationships. Particullarly within the class of gentry, where many sons have gone to university or worked outside of Ch'uhsien and thus come in contact with new ways largely imported from the West, there are many sons who demand new techniques in the selection of their wives. Some marry without consulting their parents at all; most request some voice in the selection. It is now common for a man to insist on seeing the girl or even meeting her in advance. This alteration in the traditional state of affairs has two significant results. First there is a weakening of the bond between mother and son as closer overt ties develop with the wife. This occurs at the expense of the older pattern, which demanded that the husband's concern be primarily for his mother and only secondarily for his wife. Second, the importance of the mother as a prime mover in organizing the marriage is greatly reduced, even eliminated, and her place is taken by friends who are not related by blood.

MOTHER-DAUGHTER

The relationships between a mother and a daughter in the general Chinese milieu are normally quite different from the relationships between the mother-in-law and daughter-in-law. Whereas the mother's contact with her daughter is institutionally a temporary one, with only infrequent and brief encounters after marriage,[43] the relationship between mother-in-law and daughter-in-law, though usually commencing when the girl is already well past adolescence, is based on daily and intensive contact, a large area of shared interest and experience, and a certain amount of inevitable and almost institutionalized competition and conflict.

Though the education of girls in formal schools is becoming more widespread in the gentry and wealthier merchant families, the interest in such education is generally quite weak. It is felt that the most important part of a girl's education will come from her mother and other female relatives. The scope of the woman's world, if the

---

[43] The prolonged contacts mentioned in Pruitt, 1945, would be atypical in Ch'uhsien.

woman concerned is not a peasant or a pauper, is still restricted to the home and its immediate environs, or, beyond that, to visits within a fairly limited neighborhood of households. The woman of the gentry or wealthy merchant groups does not even do the marketing and rarely has as many friends as her husband. Indeed, when the friends of the husband are present in the house for dinner, the wife is most frequently absent from the table, supervising the preparation and serving the meal. When the diners catch sight of her they call for her to join them, but in most cases she demurs. She may, however, accompany the guests in a few cups of wine if there is sufficient urging. Major digressions occur at such events as weddings, funeral feasts, or New Year feasts. The mother is restricted in her quest for companionship and must, in most cases, turn inward on her family for social contacts. Under these circumstances, the relationship between mother and daughter is frequently a very warm and mutually supporting one. The relationship of the mother-in-law to the daughter-in-law, though often described in the literature in terms of hostility and aggression can be led by these same factors to a state of warmth and mutual understanding. Ch'u ran the gamut of mother-daughter relationships, including persecutions leading to attempted suicide and warm acceptances of the daughter-in-law as a daughter.

BROTHER-BROTHER

The variation in the relationships between brothers depends on more factors than we have hitherto introduced. In addition to major differences which appear along class lines, the age of the parties, the number of brothers, the precise condition and prognosis of the family fortunes, and the relationship between the wives of the brothers are all of great importance. Traditionally, the relationship between brothers is one of the foundation stones in the social structure.[44] In such novels as the *Romance of the Three Kindoms* and *All Men are Brothers* one of the techniques used for cementing great friendships is the declaration of brotherhood, and the extension of the term *ke-ke*, or older brother, to friends is still an effective technique for the display of affection and solidarity, both in speech and in the writing of letters.

In childhood, when brothers are close together in age, their relationship is often the core of their social orientation, other contacts being grafted onto their contacts with each other. This is particularly true of boys who are raised in the countryside and who are naturally more dependent on the company of each other than is the case in the city, where large numbers of children grow up in close proximity to one another. However, even in the rural area, there are many deterrents to a completely fluid relationship. Fei, for example, describes divided inheritance where property is transmitted, before the death of the father, under conditions which favor certain sons above others.[45] Similarly, the support of the aged parents may be shared by brothers,[46] and the arrangements which are made frequently end in overt friction, particularly if the wives of the sons are in competition.

Another factor, which sometimes conditions the relationship, is the frequency with which an older brother acts

44 Vide: Levy, 1949, pp. 187-190.
45 Fei, 1939, pp. 66-67.   46Ibid., p. 74.

as the agent of the mother in early disciplinary situations. Though much of the pressure which an older brother brings to bear upon a younger one consists of ridicule and scolding, it is not unusual to see an older brother of twelve or fourteen strike a brother who is two or three years his junior. Only cases of flagrant persecution will arouse parental interference; normally, the sanction of the parents is with the elder.

If the age difference between the sons is great, the relationship is almost never one of comradeship, and this holds true on all levels of society. Where the age difference is great, the brother-brother relationship is quite likely to repeat the pattern usually associated with father and son.[47] An age difference of more than one year is also likely to cause later difficulty, since the boys, in proportion to the years separating them, participate in discrete playgroups. If the boys are from wealthy families, they are likely to go through school in different classes. This is of great importance, since, as will be described below, one of the major centers of interest for the graduate remains his school class, which, organized or unorganized, continues to supply him with social contacts for a good part of his life.

Where the family property is very small or where the family is cultivating leased land and there is no provision for the transmission of leased land to more than one heir, it is often necessary to prepare for the eventual disintegration of the family unit. Of several sons, one or two may

---

[47] See, for example, the description of the relationship between Su Tung-po and his younger brother Su Cheh as described by Lin Yutang, 1947, pp. 29-30.

be expected to remain on the land. These are generally the older boys, since their labor is used gradually and normally on the farm during their own development. The younger sons will be sent, as fortune and the contacts of the father allow, to other places, some to work as apprentices, some to become servants, some in the military, some merely to explore the possibilities of the outside.

Where the family property is large, as, for example, in the case of a prosperous commercial household, there is considerable advantage to be gained from continuing unity. Unity during the lifetime of the father, with his traditional power as the head of the household *(chia-chang)*, is often difficult enough, particularly in these present days of divergent youthful ambitions. With the death of the father, the whole structure may be menaced, each grown brother pulling in a different direction, checked only by consideration for the old mother, if she is still alive. The traditional way in which such conflicts were avoided, or at least contained, was through the recognition of the oldest brother as successor to the power of the father. In Ch'u many of the largest stores were partnerships run under the direction of one of a group of brothers. The oldest brother, however, was frequently only the head of the enterprise in name, the actual functions of administration having passed into the hands of a younger and more capable man.

SISTER-SISTER

Once married, particularly if her husband's family lives in a locality remote from her birthplace, the bride returns infrequently to the bosom of her natal family. At the beginning of her marriage she may spend almost as much time at her father's house as at her husband's. But as the years slip by, she sees less and less of her original family. Thus, the relationship between sisters is temporary. For the purposes of the present book, it is well to emphasize this fact of traditional organization and contrast it with the brother-brother relationship which is structured on the recognition of the fact that the brothers will remain together, in all likelihood, for their lifetimes. The woman obtains her feeling of security and permanence from participation in a group that is hers largely through conjugal ties, her children being the only individuals in the household to whom she is related by blood.[47b] The man, on the contrary, is surrounded by kin in a home situation. In light of this fact, it seems strange that it should be the male rather than the female who is occupied with the largest body of non-related friends.

The relationship between sisters in Ch'u does not, however, always coincide with such traditional pictures as have been drawn above or presented elsewhere.[48] When the Chinese civil war was fought in southern Shantung, northern Kiangsu, northern Anhwei, and eastern Honan, Ch'u, along the line of the Tsing-p'u Railroad, was a major stopping place for the refugees from the north. During this period of fighting in the North, Ch'uhsien was the scene of extensive guerrilla and bandit activity. Much of this armed conflict fired the neighboring *hsien* of Lai-an and Ch'uen-chiao but occasionally it came as

---

[47b] There is, however, a tradition of cross-cousin marriage (MoBrDa= FaSiSon) in which the mother-in-law is an aunt (FaSi). This, a favorable marriage, is distinguished from the opposite cross-cousin marriage (FaSiDa=MoBrSon) in which the mother-in-law is a stranger. For a critical discussion of this theme see, Francis L. K. Hsu, 1945b.
[48] Levy, 1949, p. 190.   [49] Yang, 1945, pp. 63-64.

close as the Lang-ya hills, ten or fifteen *li* south of Ch'u.
With all of this fighting, the number of refugees was great.
Many of them had no place to find shelter. Having no
contacts, no relatives, no friends, beyond the area from
which they were fleeing, the refugees moved back and
forth between Pukou and Hsuchow, the southern and
northern terminals of the Tsing-p'u line at that time. In
and about railroad stations, they lived frugally on small
amounts of food which they managed to salvage, buy, beg,
earn, or steal. In some lucky instances the refugees, particularly those who were fleeing from sudden bandit or
guerrilla raids in Lai-an or Ch'uen-chiao, managed to find
haven with relatives or friends. I recorded a small but
significant number of instances in which women with their
husbands and children had taken refuge with sisters. A
number of women who lived outside of Ch'uhsien also
visited locally dwelling sisters under less urgent conditions, coming for personal reasons, often with their children. This practise was largely, but not totally, confined
to the gentry and wealthy merchant groups whereas the
refugee pattern was present primarily within the peasantry
and poorer groups.

BROTHER-SISTER

The last of the eight pivotal relationships of the nuclear
family involves the affinities of two siblings of opposite
sex. The concerns and activities of brothers and sisters,
as children, are traditionally far removed. The further
separation of these siblings being a necessary concomitant
of patrilocal marriage, the relationship between brother
and sister is generally quite neglected. Though Levy ana-
lyzes some twenty kin relationships he does not comment

on this one, nor does Lang speak of it. Martin Yang, however describes the relationship as a close one in the period from childhood to marriage but states that after marriage there is a shift, the affections of the brother now turning toward his wife.[49] In this regard, Yang is primarily concerned with the relationship between a married brother and his spinster sister. Under conditions which almost automatically require the common residence of a wife with an unmarried, sister-in-law, friction is quite understandable, particularly if there is only a small income to be shared. The relationship between married or unmarried brother and married sister is quite likely to remain warm. Though it seemed more usual for a sister to take refuge with her brother, under the war conditions described above there were brothers from the north who had come with their families to live with a married sister.

THE CHINESE FAMILY

In view of the currency of erroneous impressions concerning the general relationship of Chinese familial structure and relationships to Chinese society at large, we may pause, in light of the foregoing material, to attempt, a broader characterization of Chinese family life.

The primary social group in which the individual participates during his lifetime is usually the nuclear family. But this small family grouping is not universal in Chinese society. There are a large number of persons who become separated from their families at an early age and who spend considerable portions of their lives without contact with their parents. Many persons remain unmarried and know no relatives. In Ch'uhsien this class is best represented by certain beggars, itinerant workers, and poor farm laborers, but also has some representation in the class of store-clerks, apprentices and government workers, who spend long periods of time without specific family contact.[50]

The relationships within the nuclear family vary considerably with the occupation of members, the wealth of the group, the personalities of the individuals composing the group as well as their respective and relative ages, the degree of isolation of the group, the exposure of members of the group to Western influences, and the size of the group. The variations themselves range from the tightest mutual dependency of related individuals to practical repudiation of responsibility.

A last point has not yet been made explicit though it may be seen clearly in the data. Friendship is not merely a supplement to relationships based on kinship. It is an authentic field of intercourse in its own right. Though, at times, it serves as a complement to pre-existing kinship rights and obligations it often challenges kinship for prior loyalty. On the one hand, it often functions as a practical device for the protection of basic kin units, extending the group and dissipating potential shocks of economic, political or even psychological nature. It also, however, furnishes avenues by which familial pressures may be avoided and introduces elements which are potentially subversive of familial unity.

---

[50] We might add such individuals as children sold as slaves, though only one such instance was recorded by me in Ch'uhsien. See Pruitt, 1945, pp. 71-72.

chapter **III**

the extended family, the clan and beyond

In a minority of societies, including our own, each nuclear family stands alone as a sort of independent atom in the community, as a unit separate from all others of its kind. In the great majority, however, . . . nuclear families are aggregated, as it were, into molecules. Clusters of two, three, or more are united into larger familial groups which commonly reside together and maintain closer ties with one another than with the other families in the community.[1]

Social scientists have traditionally aligned Chinese society with the majority here referred to by Murdock. Therefore, though our goal is to push beyond the realm of kinship in this analysis of the everyday life of a Chinese community, it is necessary to review, in some detail, those relationships which the individual maintains because of some pre-existing tie based on marriage or descent. The preceeding chapter concentrated on the first line of famil-

---

1 Murdock, 1949, p. 23.

ial relationships, those implicit in the nuclear family. In this chapter I will follow the threads of kinship grouping into broader and broader fields, turning attention, first, to the extended family, second, to the clanlike structure which is called, in Chinese, *tsu,* and third, to a consideration of those kin structured relationships which fit under none of the rubrics previously named.

TYPES OF EXTENDED FAMILY

What is an extended family? Referring again to Murdock we find the statement:

The *extended family* includes two or more nuclear families united by consanguineal kinship bonds such as those between parent and child or between two siblings. In a hypothetical but typical case, for instance, such a group might embrace the families of procreation of a father and his two adult sons.[2]

More particularly, the Chinese have the

. . . *patrilocal extended family,* which includes the families of procreation of a man, his married sons, his sons's sons, etc.[3]

Extended families must be large. Such an extensive group is often held to be the ideal Chinese family type, if not the typical one. Thus, one of the earliest dissertations in English on the subject of the Chinese family includes the following passage:

Theoretically [the Chinese family] may be defined as a group of kinsfolk consisting of parents and their children living together in a single domestic establishment. Practically it is not so similar to the families of Western nations. In China a mar-

---

[2] Ibid., p. 24. (Italics in original)   [3] Ibid., p. 34. (Italics in original)

ried son seldom establishes a new home but continues to live, with his bride, in the home of his parents. When his sons marry, they and their wives, in turn, live in the same household with their parents and grandparents. Thus a Chinese family may sometimes include several generations, from the great-grandparents to the great-grandchildren. . . . In modern China, of course, a family comprising many generations is rather hard to find, even in the rural districts. The typical family of the present includes two or three generations.[4]

We shall return to the question of the universality of the large extended family in China, but first there is the problem of the forms in which it appears. Olga Lang describes two main types of extension, the stem family and the joint family.

The stem family consists of the parents, their unmarried children, and *one* married son with wife and children. The family of this type . . . can be broken, e.g., when only one of the parents is alive or the son has no children.

The joint family consists of parents, their unmarried children, their married sons (more than one) and sons' wives and children; and sometimes a fourth or fifth generation. This family too may be either complete or incomplete. In one form of the joint family the head is the father staying with his married sons; in the other form, one of the brothers (usually the eldest) presides over his married and unmarried brothers, with their wives and his and their children, and sometimes other relatives.[5]

Peasants, tenants, petty merchants and petty artisans do not display joint family organizations. Most frequently they live in nuclear families. When they do tend, following

---

[4] Su, 1922, p. 48.

[5] Lang, 1945, p. 14. Italics and parentheses hers. See also, Levy, 1949, p. 50 ff.

a period of prosperity, to enlarge, they develop in the
pattern which Lang, after the example of Frederick Le-
Play, calls "stem families." These stem families do not
consistently involve many more relationships than those
within the normal nuclear family. Moreover, those new
contacts which are added do not materially affect the picture which was presented of the nuclear family. For
example, the survival of an aged grandparent does not
usually complicate the distribution of power within the
family. The harsh life of the peasant and tenant does not
generally lead to a condition which finds a married son,
his wife and children, sharing the family land with a strong
and capable set of parents. The "stem" variety of family
does not present sufficiently discrete characteristics to warrant separate discussion. The way is thus prepared for an
analysis of the truly significant type of extended family—
the joint family. This kind of familial organization, despite its importance as an ideal unit in the Chinese gentry's
view of their own society, is not a universal in Chinese
society. It is a relatively exclusive possession of certain
Chinese classes and not, as some romanticists would have
us believe, a general Chinese characteristic.

RELATIONSHIPS IN EXTENDED FAMILIES

Whereas the relationships basic to the nuclear family
are fairly constant and number only eight, the relationships
which may be found in an extended family are quite variable and include a large number of possibilities. Many of
these occur so rarely that they need not concern us here.
Such a relationship as that between a man and his sister's
child, for example, which in many societies is more fundamental than the tie between father and son, is relegated

7 2

outside the normal confines of the extended family by the rule of patrilineality. Similarly, the convention of patrilocality makes close institutionalized relations between certain in-laws, as between father-in-law or mother-in-law and the son-in-law, almost impossible.

The most usual relationships in an extended family include those normally found in the nuclear family plus about twenty-five additional relationships.[6] Clearly there is a wealth of potential social contacts in an extended family. Instead of analyzing each type of possible relationship in the joint family, I will take two sample extended families and indicate, through them, how these relationships operate and to what degree they function to make the extended family a unit of self-sufficiency or the instrument of first recourse in any situation.

THE MO-MO FAMILY

The Mo-mo family consists of a solid nucleus of twelve persons (Fig 1a), all of whom reside permanently in Ch'u. The family, however, is not native to Ch'uhsien but arrived about thirty years ago, when the present head of the

[6] These relationships would include those between ego (male) and the following: 1. FaFa, 2. FaMo, 3. FaFaBr, 4. FaFaBrWi, 5. FaFaBrSon, 6. FaFaBrSonWi, 7. FaFaBrSonSon, 8. FaFaBrSonSonWi, 9. FaBr, 10. FaBrWi, 11. FaSi (if unwed), 12. FaBrSon, 13. FaBrSonWi, 14. FaBrSonSon, 15. FaBrSonSonWi, 16. BrWi, 17. BrSon, 18. BrDa, 19. SonSon, 20. SonSonWi, 21. SonDa, 22. SonWi, 23. FaWi (not mother, e.g., a second or secondary wife), 24. Son of 23, 25. Da of 23. The abbreviations are: Fa-father, Mo-mother, Son-son, Da-daughter, Wi-wife, Br-brother, Si-sister. FaBrSonSonWi should be read as Father's Brother's Son's Son's Wife.

Obviously not all of these possibilities can occur simultaneously unless ego was of a tremendously long lived line. All of these relationships, however, appeared normally in the extended families I observed, though the ego of reference was frequently changed. Cf. Lee and Chin, 1929, pp. 8-10, 49.

household was only a youth. The original home is in the rural outskirts of a large city in central Kiangsu. In the original place the circle of kin included both rich peasants and merchants. The expansion of the family is a thing of the last two generations. Today, the Mo-mos in Ch'u still maintain extensive connections with the original home and also with additional family branches in several large commercial cities in other parts of Kiangsu. There is considerable mobility of family members and persons representing one branch are always visiting at some other place.

Within the group of twelve individuals which is the Mo-mo joint family, as shown on Figure 1, the following relationships may be found: FaBr-FaSon, FaBr-FaDa, FaBrWi-FaSon, FaBr-FaDa, FaSon-FaBrSon, and FaSon-FaBrDa. The frequent visits of relatives, made possible by the surplus of money, food, and living space which accompanied rich merchant status, made active certain further relationships, such as FaMo-FaDa, FaMo-FaSon, and FaBrDa-FaDa. Should this family continue to exist without splitting, there is good likelihood that another decade will see almost all of the twenty-four relationships in action.[7]

The people in Ch'u whose family name *(hsing)* is Mo-mo and who consider themselves related, are divided into two large households and are occupied in diverse but complementary fields of commerce (Fig. 1b). In fact, the specific joint family which is our immediate concern, has practical financial control over the second branch. Though

---

[7] I have since had news that the Mo-mo family underwent great change with the arrival of the new government. Apparently most of the wealthy family members fled from Ch'u.

the two sections dwell apart the separateness is difficult of precise delineation because the extended family group which is our prime concern (Fig. 1a) is itself not housed in one structure but since 1948 has occupied two houses which are perhaps fifty yards apart and on two different streets. All of the people whose *hsing* is Mo-mo and who consider themselves related are located within a radius of about two hundred yards. They live in five houses which are scattered about on four different streets. How can it be determined where one family begins and another ends?

First, it must be stressed that each of the nuclear families that goes into the composition of a larger unit has a certain life of its own. It holds for itself one or two rooms of a larger house. It owns most of the furnishings in its own rooms. Complete privacy is virtually unknown in the houses of Ch'u but admission to those rooms which are associated with a specific nuclear family is limited to the members of that family. During the day there is a good deal of free movement all about the house; more privacy is had in the night when one visits through invitation.

Second, though the Mo-mo houses show very strong ties to one another, primary loyalties tend to fall within nuclear families. This is most evident in the association of a woman with her children and the sleeping together of husband and wife. It is much less evident in the pattern of the mens' associations and in the groupings of children who have reached the age of free play.

Third, it is the nuclear family which, in certain ways, functions as the basic economic unit. While it is true that in the essentials of wealth production and in the consumption of food the basic unit is the large household, the nuclear family is important as the unit of clothing production and purchase and it is, to a large extent, the unit of recreation and luxury expenditure.

Finally, each nuclear family within a larger extended grouping recognizes its individuality and separate nature. Any Chinese informant who has participated in an extended family system can readily describe the limits, first, of his own nuclear family, beyond that, of the extended family, and lastly, of any further extensions which may be present.

In a similar fashion the joint family, which is the product of the combination of several smaller family units, may have its limits set. It is associated with the ownership of property, not only territories but commercial or financial properties as well. It is identified by a nexus of constant relationships, many of them of the type listed above. In addition, the joint family includes a number of informal contacts based on the frequency of face-to-face meetings. Further, the persons of the related small families tend to associate with each other more than they associate with the outside. This is particularly true of women, whose contacts with each other in the household far outweigh friendships which are cultivated with outside individuals. For adult men, such a generalization would not be as valid. As is shown in a later chapter, the character of a man's daily life necessitates and prepares the way for a preponderant number of external relationships. Finally, as in the case of the nuclear family, the extended family identifies itself quite self-consciously as a unit. In many cases (the Mo-mo family is one) it is referred to as *the* family by its members who, in this instance, look beyond the nuclear family to the next higher level of organization.

Within the pattern of normal everyday behavior, the

relationships which serve as binding forces are apparent. The related nuclear families of the Mo-mo group in question occupy space in two houses. The buildings are owned, not by single individuals or even by the discrete nuclear families, but by the extended family as a unit. The ownership is vested in the combined persons of the adult males, but the property is controlled and administered by a single individual, the oldest male, who in this case is the paternal uncle of the other adult males. Control and administration of the houses and property involves many things. The head of the extended family *(chia chang)* represents the whole group to the society at large. His position as the head of the family is recognized by the formal political structure in Ch'u, in the province, and in the nation. From this point of view, the office consists mainly of responsibilities such as tax payment, the reporting of population data, and social control. On the credit side, from the point of view of the individual, the office returns prestige and endows the manipulations of the *chia-chang* with a certain formal sanction. The *chia-chang* of the Mo-mo family also had several additional prerogatives. He had ultimate responsibility and power in the commercial decisions that had to be made. He was the final arbiter of budgetary questions in the household. He represented the interests of the group in the guild. His was the executive position in the family's stores. He set the time of labor, and controlled the inventory, the observations on the market, and the manipulation of transport, among other things.

The limitations on the power of the family head are visible in the Mo-mo family. The nephews had many rights which were analogous to those of partners in Western enterprises. They could veto his proposed actions or suggest courses which he was expected to follow, or at least consider. Both of these powers were exercised informally. For example, the *chia-chang* wished to erect a one-storied building to house a new venture in which the Mo-mos held a prominent interest. The nephews objected and suggested instead, that the new building be of two stories, big enough to furnish the family with additional living space. Conferences and discussions went on as part of the day's normal conversation, over the dinner table and at odd moments during the day. After a short resistance, the uncle conceded. The entire affair was conducted and ended in good humor. Issues such as these, however, can easily lead to rivalry, dissatisfaction and ultimate splitting.

The family head has powers beyond those recognized by the formal political and legal structure. Those powers which are recognized are those which stem from his biological relationship to the group of clustered kin. But the *chia-chang* of a merchant family, such as Mo-mo, lives in the midst of a large household which includes several times as many non-related folk as kin. It is not as a family head or *chia-chang* that Mr. Mo-mo formally exercised civil control over the staff of his large 'grocery' store. In that capacity he had another title, that of household-head *(hu-chang)*. Actually, very little was thought in the local community about the effectiveness of the position of *hu-chang*. Mr. Mo-mo's authority stemmed from the fact that he was the head of a big family and that he was the director of its enterprises. The smallest political position of power recognized by the populace is that of *pao-chang*, the elected official who regulated a number of families, ideally ten but frequently more.

The position of the head of the Mo-mo family was recognized in many ways. In his absence, all, even his nephews, referred to him as the "big master" *(ta lao-pan)*, an honorific title which refers to a person of some economic or political power.[8] Mr. Mo-mo was addressed as *lao-pan* by many of his customers, and all of his clerks, apprentices and servants. His nephews rarely addressed him by that title and then only when it was necessary to call to him in the shop. Otherwise, the nephews addressed him with a kinship term though, most often, they preferred to avoid direct appelation.

The position of *chia-chang* received other recognition. The uncle's clothing was finer than that worn by his nephews and he enjoyed a larger wardrobe. The room in which he lived with his wife and youngest child was superior, being quite cool in summer. It was also one of the few rooms in all Ch'uhsien which was screened against flies and mosquitos. The rooms of the nephews sported no comparable luxuries. The uncle perfomed no visible labor. The nephews were engaged in making change, entering accounts or even, on occasion, serving behind the counter, but the uncle rarely appeared in the front part of the store except to stand there, quietly, with his hands folded behind his back, checking on the general operation of the place. Most of the uncle's business was transacted in a small office behind the store. This office also served

---

[8] The term is a relative one. It may be used by beggars when soliciting alms from a patron who is himself quite poor.

as a spare bedroom, the family shrine, and the banquet rooms. Here the *lao-pan* conducted interviews with bankers, boat-men, guild representatives, and workers. With those of high status he drank wine and ate fancy dishes; with the lowly he generally sat in a chair and scowled, while the visitor stood, fidgeting, in the doorway.

The uncle arranged the precise time when one of the nephews would go off to visit the ancestral home or another branch of the Mo-mo's. He gave travel instructions and set limits on the length of the stay. He sent gifts representing the family, as well as messages and details of future plans. The uncle, himself, went back to the ancestral home only rarely, years having passed since his last visit. Instead, he preferred to be visited. When he did return to the ancestral home, his visits were short and businesslike. As a host, however, he was exceptionally considerate.

On the distaff side of this Mo-mo family, the wife of the uncle was the recognized leader. The mother of five living children, she was in robust health and relatively young. Though she was moderately conversant with the state of her husband's and the family's business affairs, she displayed little overt interest in the shops. She never played any active role in the commercial household but confined herself to the supervision of her children, the servants, and the assiduous cultivation of the game of *ma-chiang*. She spent most of her time in the company of the nephews' wives. One of these women, who was the mother of two sons, she treated with great affection. The other, who was young, very pretty, and still childless, she accepted with coolness. The two nephews' wives were frequently at odds and sometimes erupted into plate-throwing violence. In these encounters the older woman encouraged her favorite and blamed the younger woman.

Mrs. Mo-mo played *ma-chiang* almost every day from mid-afternoon until late at night. Her partners were frequently selected from among the artisans associated with the 'grocery' store. Thus, her closest acquaintances included the head baker and the man in charge of the manufacture of condiments, two persons who were unrelated members of the larger household.

Each wife was responsible for the maintenance of the family quarters of her respective nuclear family. This meant only the supervision of the servant or apprentice who was entrusted with the light daily sweeping and change of chamberpots. She was also responsible for the maintenance of the family wardrobe, making certain things such as cloth shoes herself, and supervising the tailor when one was employed. She did not prepare the family food, since that was a function delegated to a male specialist, who prepared all the meals for the entire household.

Only rarely did the nuclear families sup together as units. In this respect, non-kin ties were of greater effect than relationships based on blood or marriage. Ordinarily, throughout the store, the procedure in eating was as follows: the most important individuals in the household were the three adult males of the Mo-mo family and they sat at the first table. This was set up, in summer, in the rear of the store, and in winter, in the family shrine. Since the table at which the food was served was quite large, it could comfortably accommodate eight people. At this table ate the three men mentioned above, the accountant of the store, the oldest clerk, who was in his sixties, another clerk who was also a Mo-mo, and the present writer. One place was generally vacant, a fact of some importance, since it indicates that any individual who was not at the table was absent for some other reason than the lack of space. Only four of the regular diners were related. The other diners shared the table because of non-kin ties with the host. At the other tables the non-kin principle was even stronger. At various places in the store, groups of workers, women, servants or specialists would gather for their meals. Only one table had a rather strict kin basis and that was the one at which the women ate with their children. However, even here, the women were frequently joined by friends and acquaintances for pleasant discourses over the rice bowls.

At certain times during the year, at New Year or the eight month festival, among others, there is a ceremonial dinner, religious observances, or both. The most impressive and lengthy observance takes place during the New Year festivities. At this time family connections receive maximum stress but the effect of non-kin orientations is still remarkably strong. Thus, on the eve of the New Year holiday period, the preparations for religious worship of the household deities are assiduously overseen by Mr. Mo-mo, the family head, who makes personally certain of the sacrifices, the incense, the fireworks, and the timing of the ritual while his wife works with the cooks in the preparation of the banquet which is to come.

When devotion was made to the spirits of wealth and fortune, the order in which persons approached the altar to make their *k'o-t'ou* was significantly based on kinship but had non-kin additions. First came Mr. Mo-mo, followed by his nephews, his sons, his wife, the nephews' wives, and then the store hierarchy, starting with the old accountant and working down to the youngest apprentice. The New Year ritual was the only one carefully observed by Mr. Mo-mo and his nephews. Other rites, which were of lesser importance, were left largely in the hands of subordinate individuals. The harvest festival, for example, saw a servant setting out the sacrifice to the moon with no attention payed by any member of the family except Mr. Mo-mo who made a perfunctory first *k'o-t'ou* and walked away.

When trouble comes, family connections grow in importance. There is, however, no hard and fast rule which dictates the help which flows along kin lines. Within a society as large and complex as that of Ch'uhsien and within a culture as huge and diversified as the Chinese, no single set of standards may be said to cover even a single large community, to say nothing of the sprawling nation. Some examples will show ways that are perhaps not typical but which are at least common.

We may compare the attitudes of the Mo-mo family in the illness of a relative and of a worker. The relative was the young son of a paternal cousin of Mr. Mo-mo. The boy was thirteen years old and a close playmate of Mr. Mo-mo's two sons. He was suddenly taken sick with symptoms alarmingly suggestive of acute appendicitis. A local, Shanghai-trained doctor of Western medicine said that the boy should be taken to Nanking for an immediate operation. The Mo-mo family was distressed, knowing that bedspace in Nanking hospitals was at a premium. My aid, as a member of the household, was enlisted by Mr. Mo-mo and the boy's admission to Nanking Hospital was secured through the good offices of Dr. Daniels of that institution.

The boy was taken to Nanking by ricksha and first class train. His mother was installed in a nearby hotel. She wanted to sleep on the floor next to the boy's bed but this was discouraged by the hospital staff. It was discovered that the malady had been improperly diagnosed. Instead of appendicitis the boy had a tubercular condition of the hip. Still uncured after several weeks at the hospital, he was discharged at the request of Mr. Mo-mo, who believed that anything less than an immediate cure only reflected the inadequacy of the treatment. In Ch'u the boy received daily injections of penicillin and though the writer has no knowledge of the medical process, the boy seemed to make a splendid recovery.

Contrasted with this case, in which no effort was refused until the patient recovered, was the care, or lack of it, which was received by the first cook of the Mo-mo household. This man had obtained his position because he came from the Mo-mo native place, where he had intermediate contacts with the Mo-mos. Though very well liked by various members of the family, he was in no way related to them by blood or marriage. Some years before he had suffered a severe hernia. Chronic strain of the affected area finally brought about a serious condition. The man was permitted to refrain from work for several weeks and Mr. Mo-Mo sought, in various ways, to make him comfortable. He was moved to a cool place and an apprentice was instructed to care for his needs. No doctor was called because the man did not wish to "waste" his money. Mr. Mo-mo felt no obligation to supply the cook with medical treatment. The man, it was said, would recover, as he had done before, by resting and then by working a light schedule. When I left Ch'u for the last time, the man was working again. Though he tired easily, he seemed to ignore his condition except that it formed the main topic of his conversations and complaints.

THE CHANG FAMILY

The Chang family was not, like the Mo-mo family, commercial in its major interests. The wealth of the Chang family was in land-holdings, which were declining rapidly under the stress of inflation and the general deterioration of the Chinese national economy. The family income was supplemented by certain of its members who received wages from the government for the official posts they held. The highest such post was that of a bureau secretary in the county government. These cash increments, however, were relatively minute and each year the family had to sell or mortgage additional sections of property in order to acquire enough money for operation. Unlike the Mo-mo family, the Chang family had a long history in Ch'uhsien and had produced many scholars.

The Chang family (Fig. 2) occupied one large house which was composed of two interlocking sections, each of which fronted upon a different street. The two families had once considered themselves as one. With the death of the patriarch in 1925, there had been a splitting. The result was that each section now owned a definite portion of the ancestral lands, operated on independent budgets and considered themselves more or less discrete. The "Chang" section lived on one street and the "Chang-2" section lived on the other. One indication of the separation was the fact that visitors to one section or the other always called at the front gate of the respective houses on the proper street, a decided inconvenience. The household members, however, still continually, if not habitually, felt free to move through either house. Indeed, as the old women were fond of pointing out, relations between the two sections were becoming better with passing years, having improved steadily after the split when hostilities had been quite overt.

The composition of the two sections at the beginning of 1947 was as follows: The 'Chang' house included its paternal grandmother, the wife of the deceased Mr. Chang, three unmarried sons of the dead Mr. Chang, the wife of the eldest son, who was himself absent, living in Shanghai, and his infant son. One female servant completed this household. In 1948 the paternal grandmother died, reducing the total by one. A number of quartered soldiers who lived in the 'Chang' house in 1948 were never considered household members. The 'Chang-2' household included two elderly women, the wives of the deceased nephews of the old Chang grandmother. The first woman had two married sons who lived in the household with their wives and children. The second woman had four sons, two of whom lived with the household in Ch'u, one of them with his wife and two children, the other with his childless bride. Two sons were living away from Ch'u but their wives and children remained in the 'Chang-2' household. The number of related persons was twenty, and there were two female servants.

The 'Chang-2' house was larger than the 'Chang' house; the latter had five units *(chien)* of rooms, whereas the former had seven. The total *chien* of twelve rooms is a large number and gives some idea of the wealth and power of the Chang family before its split. The 'Chang-2' family was the one which included the county official, hence it escaped the inconvenience of domiciling soldiers.

The nominal head of the 'Chang' household was a young man, twenty-eight years old, a graduate of a college in southwestern China during the Japanese War. Actually, the power in the household was wielded by his mother, a capable woman of about fifty. Conditions in the 'Chang' household were such that the family constantly verged on financial collapse. Mr. Chang, who was responsible for the collection of rents on the family lands, abhorred the job. He was greatly influenced by liberal currents of political thought and no longer was certain of the right of a land-lord to extract rent from the tenants. His own inability to deal with financial transactions stood him in bad stead and his diary was filled with plaintive notes about the evil of money. Since financial matters were the main topic of conversation at home, he spent the bulk of his time with friends or acquaintances and avoided as many painful discussions as possible.

Mr. Chang's two younger brothers were students in a Ch'u middle-school. Paying for their education was a ma-jor drain on the family resources, but the continuation of these boys in school was never questioned. The problem was to guarantee them entry into a college and Mr. Chang and his mother were continually estimating how the land could be mortgaged best for this purpose. In fact, Mr. Chang had given up, for an indefinite period of time, the thought of marriage. He had met a girl in Szechuan during the war and desired to send for her. However, the burden this would have put upon his own family budget made it impossible and in letters from Szechuan, the girl revealed that she was essential to the support of her own family, since she was an elementary school teacher.

The 'Chang' and 'Chang-2' sections each took full and complete control of the basic food, clothing, and shelter needs of its members. The 'Chang' family represents, in its structure, a somewhat distorted extended family. At one time it displayed four generations living together simultaneously. At the death of the paternal grandmother it returned to three generations. The fact that four generations managed to live together for a full year was very important to the family and they sat for a group portrait to commemorate the event. The aged grandmother was, however, a great burden to the family. So much so that Mr. Chang looked forward to her death. Though the performance of the burial rites, after her demise, was carried out at almost ruinous expense, the prestige gained from the year of living with four generations together was a source of much satisfaction.

In obtaining the basic essentials of life, the role of the extended family is clear. Most of the essentials were not produced by the labor of any individuals in the household. No food was grown, few clothes were made, and no person related to the Changs knew how to build a house. The family, however, was the unit of ownership of strategic wealth. By this I mean that the ownership of those properties from which the income of the family was largely derived was vested in the family as a unit. Unfortunately, the example of the 'Chang' family does not show this clearly, since it lacks clear-cut nuclear families within its larger structure. A glance at Fig. 2 will show, however, that in the 'Chang-2' family there were at least three complete nuclear families embodied in the larger organization.

Those nuclear families maintained separate economies only in the most insignificant details. For instance, the children of those nuclear families might receive extra little toys from their own parents, they might be dressed in finer clothes or their parents might themselves indulge in extra luxuries. In basic matters, the extended family was the unit of supply. The house was of the extended family; the meals were prepared for the whole family by the women and the servants; most of the clothing was allotted on a *pro-rata* basis, etc.

Despite this view of the extended family as a tight and well-functioning unit in the society, it is important to remember that the family acts mainly as an agency connecting individuals with the larger civil society. It is necessary to point out that only rarely within classes which are associated with joint families is any productive function vested in the family. All of these joint families, in other words, extract their subsistence from the manipulation of people, not the manipulation of tools and materials. In the case of the Changs, this is done primarily through the exploitation of land rights which, until now, has been so much a part of Chinese culture. With the Mo-mo family previously described the basis of subsistence lay in techniques of exploitation of a large local market, and to a degree, of local labor power. It will be of great interest to follow future developments in China on this point. Since the old concept of landlords' rights is theoretically being banished, it seems likely that the joint family will suffer severe maladjustments which might lead to its disappearance. On the other hand, the present adoption by the Chinese Communists of a "New Economic Policy," resembling the Russian experiment of 1922-28, will tend to maintain the merchants in their family system.

The extended family is not always a peaceful unit of cooperation. Splitting, of course, represents the most acute phase of disharmony, but there are many varieties of chronic friction which require constant arbitration. In Ch'u of 1947-48, the gentry, most of whom were caught in a vise of rising prices and declining income, were frequently divided within their various families over the problems of ceremonial expenditures. In the three major crisis rites, birth, marriage, and death, there are many rituals and ceremonies whose proper fulfillment is possible only at great financial cost. Mr. Chang was twice caught in such problems.

When his sister-in-law's child was born, Mr. Chang succeeded in reducing the 'third-day-party' *(kuo san jih)*[9] from a banquet to a small affair. The sister-in-law, normally a placid person, was incensed. When the child reached his first birthday Mr. Chang was subjected to unceasing argument until, finally, the birthday was celebrated with much pomp and expenditure. In this fight Mr. Chang was opposed by his sister-in-law, his mother, and most of the adults in the 'Chang-2' household; allied with him were all of his friends and one young man of the 'Chang-2' family who was much like our Mr. Chang and who had, in his turn, lost similar battles in his own household.

While Mr. Chang's old paternal grandmother was alive, the family basked in the glory of its four generations. The

---

[9] See Yang, 1945, p. 123.

old woman was a weight on the family budget. She was getting medication and treatment from a Western-trained doctor at Mr. Chang's insistence, though in order to quiet the old lady's fears, several old fashioned doctors were in consultation. Mr. Chang was much perturbed. He was under constant pressure from his mother to assure her that he would give his grandmother the finest possible funeral. The mother was under pressure herself from the 'Chang-2' household and from related Changs throughout Ch'u. Mr. Chang was encouraged by his close circle of friends to resist 'superstition' and stand fast against old fashioned ways. Mr. Chang swore that he would not budge, though he noted that each of his friends had, in their turn, surrendered when faced by a similar crisis.

Finally the old lady died and Mr. Chang immediately began to prepare a lavish funeral. He spent almost his entire available reserve on a coffin, on paper offerings, scrolls, and the other accoutrements of the funeral. When asked about his former statements he said that he was only trying to satisfy his mother. He also said that he would be unable to face or live with his relatives unless he did this thing properly. But when the time came to get together more money to hire musicians and pay the horde of people necessary to carry sacrifices and ritual paraphernalia, Mr. Chang discovered that he had reached the end of his economic tether. His relatives, instead of sending cash as funeral gifts, had contented themselves with sending scrolls which bore well composed messages of condolence. Some relatives, quite shameless, Mr. Chang told me, had sent only the cheapest of ghost money as an offering. Mr. Chang could pawn no more land, for it was set aside for the education of his brothers. Not even his mother could object to that. He canvassed his relatives for loans. Small amounts were reluctantly offered and had to be accepted. The director of the county bank, a rather distant relative, was approached and he offered a loan at exceptionally good terms but the amount was pitifully small. Each day, after trying to get more money, Mr. Chang would bitterly repeat the Chinese proverb, "Nearby neighbors are worth more than distant relatives."[10]

In Mr. Chang's case the proverb seemed to contain a good deal of truth. Not only did nearby friends respond to his needs with more alacrity than distant relatives, but they outdid nearby relatives as well. Most of the money that had come from relatives had been advanced as personal loans, some even requiring small interest payments, but the amounts that came from friends were, in many instances, gifts, with the tacit understanding that repayment would be essayed only when Mr. Chang's financial position had materially improved.

Detailed discussion of the various crisis rites in which the extended family engages as a unit would be out of place in the present analysis. The fact is that most of the crisis rites are clearly oriented about blood relationships. The key guests are relatives, the most prominent roles are often played by relatives, and the ritual emphasizes the role and function of family organization. However, in all cases, the role of non-kin relationships is great and may not be overlooked. At birth, and in the ceremonies commemorating birth, outsiders play a prominent part. The

---

[10] Chinese proverbs, like English ones, are often contradictory. Compare, "Let each man sweep away the snow from his own doorstep without heeding the frost on his neighbor's roof."

arrangements leading to marriage are often in the hands of non-related individuals, go-betweens who act either in a professional capacity or for the pleasure and prestige of the task.[11] At the marriage ceremonies the most crucial rites are those which concern the ancestors of the groom, but there are many points during the course of the ceremony at which the importance of non-related persons is stressed.[12] The funeral, most impressive of family affairs, also has many points of external orientation. One commentator, for example, notes that in southeastern China it was the custom to invite high ranking officials to the encoffining. A notable was to drive the first nail into the casket in order to insure the success of future generations.[13] In Ch'u it is highly desirable that as many prominent citizens as possible attend the funeral.

THE CLAN

The grouping which unites a number of extended families into a functioning body is called a *tsu*. This patrilineal assemblage of kindred shows many resemblances to the phenomenon usually labelled 'clan' in the anthropological literature.[14] The *tsu* has received a good deal of attention, both descriptively and analytically,[15] hence, the present treatment will be brief and to the point of establishing

---

[11] See Lau Shaw's, *The Quest for Love of Lao Lee*, 1948, for an amusing description of an amateur go-between.

[12] Vide: Lang, 1945, p. 38; Werner, 1919, pp. 46-51, shows much of the outward orientation of the wedding with its display aimed at impressing the community at large.

[13] De Groot, 1892, vol. I, pp. 96-97.

[14] Whereas such scholars as Lowie use the Chinese as exemplifying a type of clan structure (Lowie, 1948, pp. 236-237), others, notably Murdock (Murdock, 1949, Table 66, p. 237) deny clans to the Chinese.

[15] Hu, 1948; Lang, 1945, Chap. XV; Levy, 1949, *passim, etc.*

those social functions which are relegated to this form of organization.

From Hu Hsien-chin we may note the significant functions of the *tsu* or of its smaller subdivision, the *fang*. In the religious sphere, the clan is concerned with the maintenance of rites which honor the clan ancestors. It is also responsible for the condition of the ancestral shrine. While this function cannot be under-estimated as a matter close to the heart of the normal *tsu* member, it is well to note that Chinese religious practice on the lay level does not ordinarily reveal the factors of compulsion and obsession which are so often encountered in the West. Thus, in central China, ancestral halls are frequently found to be in a state of decay, shrines serve as lodgings or dining halls, or the building, which is the focus of ancestral rites, will be rented out as a dwelling to a tenant farmer, often a non-relative.

Vitally connected with ancestral veneration is the matter of the care of the dead. In Ch'u there is only one *tsu,* which has an elaborate procedure for the care of the graves of the *tsu* members. This *tsu* has a central burial ground located some miles out of South Gate. The graves are surrounded by a handsome copse of trees and is one of the beauty spots in this part of the county.[16] Most of the other *tsu* of Ch'uhsien do not have common burial grounds. Not only is it usual for each family, nuclear or extended, depending on the family fortunes and class position, to take care of its own burials but, in most cases, persons will be buried separately, even husbands and wives, the geomancer making a new and individual attempt to

---

16 Compare, Hu, 1948, p. 37ff.   17 Hu, 1948, pp. 65-70.

find the best location for each grave. Thus, in Ch'u, the focus of after-death activities is in the family rather than in the clan.

Religious functions in the clan cannot be clearly separated from economic powers. The maintenance of the ancestral shrine, even when in a condition of decay, generally carries with it the right to profit from the control of certain ancestral properties.[17] Not all of the revenue from the clan lands goes into temple maintenance. Much of it, depending on the local circumstances, may be used to feather the comptroller's nest.[18] In Ch'u the most important social function of the surplus from clan lands is to provide a fund for the education of young clan members.[19] Thus, the component families of a *tsu* called Li, which owned much land outside of East Gate, were far from equal in wealth. Some of the joint families which composed the larger social unit owned extensive lands which were rented to tenants, and one of the wealthier families had a member in a relatively high post in the National government. Other families within the Li *tsu* had, however, great financial difficulties and, like the 'Chang' family described above, had to resort to land sales to maintain themselves. In one such family the son, a bright lad of nineteen, was being sponsored in his education by the *tsu*. His scholastic record, however, was quite poor and, through lack of interest, he was deficient in certain subjects which were crucial in entrance examinations. The *tsu* had great difficulty in finding a college which would accept him. The influential relative worked

---

[18] Chen Han-seng, 1936, Ch. II.
[19] On clan subsidies for education see Hu, 1945, p. 77ff.

zealously through his political and social contacts and admittance to a Nanking institution was finally secured. The actual responsibility for the appointment, by this time, rested in hands known hardly even to the first influential relative. A chain of non-kin contacts had been mobilized by an original kin stimulus.

The political sanctions by which a *tsu* may attempt to control its membership are quite varied.[20] The major punishment is loss of the benefits of *tsu* membership.[21] This does not necessarily imply ostracism but only loss of claim to certain positive advantages such as educational subsidy and preference as a tenant. At any rate, in central China, particularly in the community of Ch'uhsien, such a sanction is mild to the point of impotence and reflects the exceptionally weak development of the clan in this area.

BEYOND THE CLAN

In a patrilineally organized society, kin relationships which are 'beyond the clan' include ties on the maternal side many of which link individuals of close biological connection. There are also a number of ties which result from marriage. The tie of a man to his maternal uncle, or his tie to his wife's brother are equally distinct from ties within the *tsu*. Such relationships are quite difficult to describe, since they lack institutionalization and present few sweeping regularities on which generalizations may be based. They may not, however, be omitted since in individual cases they may be of great value.

In Lin Yueh-hwa's study of familism in Fukien, the two

---

20 Hu, 1945, p. 59ff, Appendices 26, 28, 29, 30, 31.   21 Ibid, p. 61.

major families in the discussion are the Changs and the Hwangs. United in business friendship and mutual dependence, the two houses were linked by an original relationship based not upon clan kinship but on the ties of marriage; the two family heads were brothers-in-law.[22] Examples of dependence and affection based on similar ties may also be given from Ch'u. In one family, the brother-in-law was a central figure. A petty government official in Nanking, he spent much of his time attending to the affairs of his wife's family in Ch'uhsien. Strongwilled and with a flair for business, he took much of the load of financial affairs from the shoulders of his brother-in-law, a scholar, who was the nominal family head. In return, the children of the brother-in-law lived in Ch'u under the care of their maternal grandmother. Similarly, in the family world of the Mo-mo's, who have already been discussed, there were many examples of 'beyond clan' relationships. Several clerks were introduced into the store hierarchy by the wife of the older Mo-mo. One of the most important men in the Mo-mo business organization was a maternal relative whose job it was to explore new commercial possibilities in Shanghai and other cities. Precise patterns, however, were lacking and for each instance of cooperation among such relatives, many more cases of complete lack of contact between these relatives could be presented.

REPRISE

Some of the major social ties which flow from kin considerations have now been introduced. At this point we may state certain tentative general conclusions.

---

[22] Lin Yueh-hwa, 1947.

Many individuals on the Chinese social scene do not live in any of the groupings that have, as yet, been mentioned. The very poor are often found living as individuals; frequently they do not marry, and sometimes they do not become members of families of procreation. Clerks in town enterprises, though originating and often continuing membership in nuclear families, spend much of their time isolated from those families. Where the fact of nuclear family membership is established, the patterns which are implied fall short of universality. Procreation is the single most important function of the nuclear family. This holds regardless of class level. Such is not the case in the matters of subsistence, religious life, education or recreation. In each of these categories functions which in many cultures are normally associated with the nuclear family may be found in China to be associated with joint families or with the *tsu*.

The nuclear family is the basic unit for the great majority of tenants, peasants, petty merchants, and artisans and, in general, for those individuals who have small supluses, or none at all, and little opportunity for amassing wealth. Among these types the nuclear family serves as the instrument of wealth production and distribution. It is the social organ into which the young are born and which cares for those who have died. It is a first recourse in times of trouble or stress. It is the primary unit of recreation and, for many, the practical classroom in which they get the bulk of their education. Though, as we shall see, no family in Ch'u is economically, politically, or religiously a unit unto itself, in each of these areas the first focus is within the nuclear family.

The joint family is the most prevalent and most important kind of extended family. It is a possession of the more economically successful members of the community, the big merchants, landlords and officials. Where the extended family exists, the nuclear family suffers a limitation of function. Many of its classic operations are taken over by the larger grouping. Thus, the quest for subsistence, the accumulation of wealth, the distribution of the surplus, the allocation of political power, and the care of the young, among other things, rest in the wealthier classes, with the joint families.

Finally, the broadest systems of kinship, the patrilineal clan and the matrilineal and conjugal relatives, especially in Ch'u, vary widely in practical function and frequently lag in importance. More or less stress may be laid upon these types of kin connection in individual cases. Rarely, however, do any of these types take the center of the stage in the patterning of behavior or the alignment of basic social relationships.

chapter **IV**

extra-kin forces in an agricultural milieu

The preceding chapters have dealt at some length with the nature of kinship ties in the social structure of Ch'uhsien. I have tried to indicate the nature of the basic relationships which one normally finds within the nuclear family, the extended family and, to some extent, the clan and beyond. This has set the stage for a consideration of those elements which lie at the heart of the matter, the structured relationships which revolve about friendship or some non-kin tie.

Most of Ch'uhsien's farmers when compared with the gardeners of the area are seen to be engaged in an extensive type of cultivation, planting staple crops such as wheat, rice, corn and beans. It may strike the casual reader who is accustomed to the description of all Chinese farming as intensive, that the field farmer, in this study is described as "extensive." The distinction is based on a large register of facts, a detailed analysis of which is not necessary to the present book. Among the most important, however, are the following. The unit of cultivation in gardening is a strip of land which generally averages one-fortieth or one-fiftieth of an acre. The size of the typical field unit, on the other hand, is rarely more than one-sixth of an acre and generally is about one-twelfth or one-eighteenth of an acre. The crops grown in gardens are largely vegetables, roots, and beans. The predominant field crops are grains. The garden is tilled exclusively with human labor. The field is often worked with water buffalo. The tools used in the garden are specialized for ultra-intensive cultivation. The field implements are larger and include the plow.

Our major concern with the Ch'uhsien field-farm family is in its extensive involvement in ties that transcend kinship. There are many functions which such non-kin ties serve. There are ties which assure production. There are relationships which furnish techniques of relieving farm labor shortages and surpluses. There are contacts which are used to broaden the economic area from which income may be derived, or income supplemented. There are also a number of non-kin relationships which underlie tenancy as a form of land tenure, and many connections which flow from the existence of a state which makes many demands on the farmers. All of these areas of relationships are basic to elementary survival. They precede relationships which involve religious, educational, or recreational adaptations. Thus, I shall first investigate relationships which may be termed, in a broad sense, economic, and then turn to the other areas of contact which have been mentioned.

The first concern of the farmer is for his land. Though the percentages of tenancy differ in the various areas of

China,[1] tenancy is widespread in Ch'uhsien. During the period of my residence two factors operated in tandem to promote tenancy throughout the county. The lands lying nearest the city wall were of the greatest value since they were most accessible to markets and transient supplies of labor. The more remote lands were largely outside the realm of protection of the garrison in Ch'u and wealthy landlords ran great risks in exposing themselves in the countryside. A third reason for the large extent of tenancy in this area may possibly be found in the effects of the Taiping warfare. So many people were destroyed or permanently dislocated in the Ch'uhsien area, as the result of the Taiping rebellion, that the survivors found themselves, or manoeuvered themselves into the ownership of relatively large estates. For a number of reasons these estates proved of optimum value when divided among a number of tenants rather than being worked by the owner and his family.

From the statistical work of Buck and the limited sampling I was enabled to perform in Ch'uhsien, I have concluded that tenancy was the major type of tenure in the area. It is of value to investigate at this point the relationships which are implicit in this type of land-holding. China has had many different types of tenancy. Among these are share cropping in which the tenant supplies only labor and the landlord gives the land, tools, house and the seed; share renting in which the tenant supplies seed and tools in addition to his labor, the landlord supplying the land and helping in the construction of the house; and cash renting in which a definite and

---

[1] Buck, 1930, p. 150.

predetermined amout of money is paid, all of the produce being kept by the farmer.[2] Ch'uhsien specializes in the share renting system. The tenant is expected to supply himself with seed, tools, and animals. He is also responsible for constructing his own house and, though the landlord may be called upon to furnish the tenant with the house poles, the tenant must supply the mud and thatch. There is, however, no hard and fast rule. If times are bad, the landlord will be asked to supply seed. Frequently this will be done on terms which are only slightly less difficult than those which are offered by the usurer. Many landlords, however, especially those who had a long and close association with their tenants, could be prevailed upon to lend grain for seed at a low rate of interest, or even none at all. Such cases of generosity were always found among landlords who were local residents; absentee landlords who lived in Nanking or Shanghai and who were represented by agencies were not identified with such munificence.

KAN-CH'ING

Rent is paid by one of two systems in Ch'uhsien. The most widespread system is based on a flat forty percent of the crop yield of the staple grains paid at each harvest, spring and fall. This system is known locally as *huo ts'u* or "flexible" (literally—"living") rent. The farmer frequently has a small part of his land in non-staple crops. For Ch'uhsien these include cotton, sweet potatoes, peas and others. The disposition of these secondary crops is not rigidly fixed. A certain amount will be presented to

---

[2] T'ang, 1924, pp. 236-38.

the landlord at each harvest and this amount, being quite variable, may be the source of much conflict between the landlord and the tenant. The landlord, if his share is too small, will take his stand on the assertion that too much land is being put into 'extra' crops and insist that their planting be curtailed. The precise balance in this situation, is determined in large measure by the quality of the relationship between the two parties, a quality which is expressed in the term *"kan-ch'ing."*[3] All contacts between persons are understood by the people of Ch'uhsien to vary in warmth and intensity. The degree of that variation among people who are unrelated is expressed in *kanch'ing,* which is always described as 'good,' 'not-bad,' not-good,' or, worst of all, 'absent.' For the most part, *kan-ch'ing* expresses a relationship between two individuals who are not on precisely the same social plane. It is possible to say that your *kan-ch'ing* with a friend of the same social level is good, but it is not likely in Ch'uhsien that you would use the word in such a way. *Kan-ch'ing* is the primary institutionalized technique by which class differences are reduced between non-related persons, or even, as we shall see below, between distantly related kin. In this respect it differs from the state of friendship which, in many cases, makes a tacit assumption of equality. *Kan-ch'ing* grows between the parties concerned and frequently is a direct variable of the length of the acquaintanceship. This factor

------

[3] The *Tzu Yuan,* a Chinese dictionary, defines *kan-ch'ing* in the following terms: "Because of external influences one is moved emotionally. Now, the resultant sentiment is called *kan-ch'ing.* If [the relationship from which the sentiment stems] is close and affectionate, the *kan-ch'ing* is said to be good. If there is jealousy and avoidance it is said that there is bad *kan-ch'ing,* etc."

is not infrequently verbalized and one hears, "I know him for a long time, our *kan-ch'ing* is good." Time alone is not the sole factor. Particularly on the agricultural level there are many things which enter into *kanch'ing*. Attempts on the part of the tenant to cheat the landlord of predetermined amounts of grain-rent will cause the relationship to deteriorate, as will continued poor harvests, excessive demands on the landlord for credit, avoidance of obligations which the landlord demands as his due, and many other actions. On the part of the landlord there is less concern for *kan-ch'ing*, since he is the power-figure in the relationship, the one whose *kan-ch'ing* is particularly desired. However, even the wealthiest landlord has a certain interest in *kan-ch'ing* because production may be spurred by it, cheating may be reduced by it, and it is only within the bounds of propriety that all relationships can be carried on properly.[4]

LAND TENURE AND RENT

To indicate more clearly the nature of *kan-ch'ing*, the methods by which it functions, and the purpose of its existence, I will present some more detailed material on the nature of the rental system in Ch'uhsien. The customary rent of forty percent of the staple crops at harvest admits of wide manipulation by skillful tenants. With their physical and intellectual separation from the land, many landlords become increasingly ignorant of farm conditions. Thus, many are not quite clear as to the normal amount of produce which they are legally entitled to

---

[4] Though the term does not appear, one report lays great stress on the value of affection of a *kan-ch'ing* type in recruiting agricultural labor, during a period of labor scarcity in Yunnan. See Fei, 1941, p. 165.

expect. Other landlords are not aware of local agricultural conditions and cannot reply when their tenants insist that the water was insufficient for rice and therefore the crop is poor. Many farmers are experts at filling the containers of rice in such a way that they appear most liberally full when they are really partly empty. It is also a skill to reduce the quality of the landlord's share by giving him a larger portion of inferior rice and, occasionally, to introduce a certain amount of foreign matter, such as pebbles, into the rice to swell its bulk. None of these tactics may be used to an extreme and the balance of wealth is never threatened by these techniques. The landlord, however, considers behavior of this sort as reprehensible since it does make petty inroads on his own subsistence and because it represents a latent disregard of the system upon which his livelihood is based. The major mechanisms which protect the landlord are two. He profits by the tenant's concern for good *kan-ch'ing*. The tenant, not knowing when some sudden emergency will leave him at the landlord's complete mercy or when he will have to go to the landlord for some favor, is cautious in his relationships with his patron. The tenant, under the weight of great insecurity, cannot tamper with the one relationship which may afford him hope in adversity.[5] The second sanction of the landlord is his power. Legally, the control of the land is almost unilaterally a function of the landlord. The political machinery of the county and, if need be, the province and even the nation, was mobilized primarily to defend this landlord control. This alignment of power is facilitated because Ch'uhsien, unlike certain areas de-

---

[5] Compare Chinese Economic Journal, 1927, p. 372.

scribed by Fei Hsiao-tung does not have a concept of divided tenure, the tenant having topsoil right and the owner having subsoil right.[6] There are only the protections of customary right and *kan-ch'ing* which ensure the tenant of his land year after year. Should the land pass from one landlord to another, the tenant may find himself dispossessed.

An interesting variation of the flexible rent system operates in the absence of the title holder from the locality. The agency which represents the title holder may be (as in most cases is the fact) a locally dwelling relative. In a minority of cases, the title-holder is represented by a purely commercial agent. The agent may also develop elaborate patterns of *kan-ch'ing* and is capable of playing the role normally held by the resident title-holder, gaining a portion of the "extra" crops and even benefiting by such customary services as the use of tenants as servants at weddings and funerals.

The second system of rent in Ch'uhsien is called *ai ts'u* or "rigid" rent and sets a fixed amount of grain to be paid semi-annually. This system operates to the advantage of the tenant in a bumper crop year but can bring about his ruin if the crop yield is low. The system is based on an estimate of the average yield; the rent is computed at forty percent of this figure and stated as a fixed volume of grain. Such a system operates to the best advantage of a landlord who has lost contact with farming and who can not rely on *kan-ch'ing* to keep his tenant in line. It is important to note that *ai ts'u* is a minority rental system in Ch'uhsien.

---

6 Chen Han-seng, 1936, p. 52; Fei, 1938; Chinese Economic Journal, 1927, pp. 87-88; Institute of Pacific Relations, 1939, p. 25-26.

Before leaving the question of land tenure and rental systems it should be pointed out that not only is the land cultivated by the farmer frequently not his own, but in an apparently overwhelming number of cases in Ch'uhsien it actually belongs to a totally unrelated individual. Thus, in satisfying his first need, which is for land to cultivate, the farmer operates beyond the most widely extended realm of kinship as he is immediately driven into intimate and prolonged contact with the civil world. We may ask, in such cases, how was the initial contact between the landlord and the tenant managed?

Prospective tenants and landlords may meet in one of three approved ways. The landlord may seek a suitable tenant, the tenant may approach the landlord, or a third party may bring the two together. It is quite difficult to estimate the relative importance of each of these categories but of the three approaches the last seems most popular. Even in those cases in which the tenant desires to approach a landlord whom he knows to be looking for a suitable tenant, the resort is to an intermediary, a procedure whch is also used in arranging marriages and settling disputes. In many cases, a person of some status, who has some previous obligation to either the prospective tenant or the landlord, now offers his services. Many landlords, for example those who have particularly good *kan-ch'ing* with their tenants, will try to get additional land for a tenant's adult son, sometimes contacting other landlords when their own land is inadequate.

In the quest for land or tenants there are very few professional go-betweens in Ch'uhsien; for such arrangements the preferred go-between is either a friend or a relative. When the landlord and tenant have met and the landlord is satisfied that the tenant is likely to be a good farmer, for which he has the assurances of the go-between, a temporary contract is drawn up for a maximum of three years. If the tenant proves satisfactory during this period, and if the landlord does not suddenly discover some more pressing obligation which would give prior right to some other individual, a long term document is drawn up and thereafter the tenant has relative security. Even with the contract, however, the tenure of the tenant is not necessarily permanent.[7] Ch'uhsien had a legal code which covered such contractual right and obligations but local arrangements did not often involve the formal legal standards. There was a tremendous resistance to anything smacking of the courtroom because court was associated with ruin and loss. Instead, custom and *kan-ch'ing* were relied upon for guidance. In this instance *kan-ch'ing* was quite important but custom was fluid, there being considerable disagreement among landlords, some of whom claimed that no tenant could be dispossessed except after a transfer of land while other landlords claimed that the tenant could be freely evicted, especially if there was good cause, e.g., fraud[7a] or incompetence. One case illuminates the contradictory nature of these statements but also shows the importance of *kan-ch'ing*. A landlord, Mr. J., had a tenant who was notoriously lazy and who began to smoke opium. This tenant cultivated an extensive section of Mr. J.'s lands, the return from which began to drop alarmingly. The tenant had a nephew who was hard working and

---

7 Compare conditions at Kwanyun, Kiangsu. Chinese Economic Journal, 1927, pp. 371-72.

7a Since attempts to withhold rent are virtually institutional, it would not be difficult to gather evidence of fraudulent practices. See above p. 105.

competent but who cultivated only a small plot of Mr. J.'s land. The relationship between Mr. J. and his tenant was excellent and as the *kan-ch'ing* between the older brother and Mr. J. grew worse the nephew improved his position. Finally Mr. J., who was completely upset over the whole matter, not having the heart to dispossess his incompetent tenant despite the advice of his own friends and relatives, solved his problem by transferring the nephew to the extensive land and putting the older man on the smaller plot.

LABOR SUPPLY AND SURPLUS

I have indicated that the first call upon the peasant's labor is had by a generally unrelated individual, his landlord. In addition to taking some two-fifths of the crops which the farmer produces, the landlord has other rights which he expects to have fulfilled. On the two major holidays, *kuo-nien* or New Year's, and *pa yüeh chieh* or the eighth month moon harvest festival, the tenant presents his landlord with choice edibles from the farm, including fowl and eggs and a store-bought cake *(yüeh ping)* for the harvest feast. The landlord is supposed to reciprocate with a feast in his house at which the tenants are guests. Though the tenant's donation continues, the feast has largely disappeared. Concern for *kan-ch'ing* is the problem primarily of the tenant. Among other demands which a tenant may be expected to fulfill is the furnishing of labor, either gratis or for a nominal sum, during the harvest to transport the grain of the *laopan* to town. During the winter slack season, a young girl or a boy may be sent to the town to act as a servant in the landlord's house. In many instances maintainence of the

servant is the only payment but, since this eases the farm
budget, it is welcomed.

The balance of labor on the farm is very delicate and
affects not only tenants but all those engaged in agriculture. The labor question is complicated by the nature of
the agricultural cycle. At certain times of the year there
is a huge demand for labor, while at other times there
is virtually nothing to do. In Ch'uhsien, as in other regions
in China,[8] the concept of labor unit is found. A man is
considered as one unit while a woman, older man, or child
is considered as half a unit. The land-labor unit, however,
shows great variation in different parts of China. Fei mentions a land-labor unit called *kung,* which varies from
place to place, in one locale being one-eighteenth acre,[9]
and in another being about one-twelfth acre.[10] In Ch'uhsien, as in at least one other locale,[11] there is a concept of
a large land unit based on animal labor. Fei does not
describe this unit beyond saying that it is called *chai* or
wagon and represents the amount of land which may be
plowed in one day with a buffalo. In Ch'uhsien there is a
similar concept which is called *i t'iao niu t'ien,* "one piece
buffalo land," generally averaging between forty and fifty
mou in area. When one asks a Ch'uhsien farmer for more
specific information he may be told, as I was, "It depends
on the size of the buffalo."

The importance of the unit of cultivation and labor
utilization for this study lies in the frequent imbalances
which occur. The family which has a sufficiency of human
labor for its property or which does not have a surplus of

---

8 Fei, 1945, pp. 30-32.   9 Fei and Chang, 1945, pp. 29-30.   10 Ibid.,
p. 137.   11 Ibid., p. 29.

labor is exceptionally rare.[11a] Instead, it is far more usual to come upon a household which must either make provision for the inclusion of additional labor units, or, equally important, make provision for the absorption of extra units in some way so that the subsistence level of the family is not threatened by virtual parasitism.[12] In addition to such pressing questions, there is the omnipresent necessity of disposing of labor surpluses caused by seasonal shifts.[13] In the attempts which are made to solve these difficulties, the family connections of the individuals concerned often play secondary roles as most of the action involves persons who have no kinship connections.

One of the primary ways in which a shortage of labor is overcome is through the institution of the hired worker. As most studies of China have pointed out, there are two basic types of hired laborer, the *ch'ang kung* or long-term laborer and the *tuan- kung* or short-term laborer. Personal relationships, as opposed to impersonal contact, are more likely to appear in the tie between the long-term worker and the farmer. Yang, writing of this relationship in a village in southern Shantung, remarks:

Generally, every family must show its hired men that it has done for them all that its economic ability permits. Otherwise the laborers complain and broadcast the fact that the family is stingy, which would make it difficult for them to get people

---

[11a] What could be more symptomatic than this of the transition from kin to civil society? Kin societies have relatively low productive demands which do not begin to test the limits of the means of production. Thus the problem of labor surplus and deficit does not appear. But when individual ownership of land occurs, such dislocations arise automatically.
[12] Cf. Institute of Pacific Relations, 1939, pp. 76-77.
[13] *Ibid,* pp. 70-71.

to work on their farms. On . . . three occasions (Ch'ing Ming, Tuan Wu, and Pa Yueh Chieh) , the farm hands are treated as guests; the head of the family pours wine for them and begs them to eat as much as they can. There is a common belief that to feed the hired men well is one of the prerequisites for the success of a family's farm management.[14]

This picture does not quite fit Ch'uhsien, being rather idyllic. It is true that in Ch'uhsien the major holidays also see the feasting of the laborers, a custom which has an interesting parallel in the town where the clerks and workers are fêted by their employers, but the daily standard of life does not justify the claim that the laborers are treated as well as the family is able. There is an interesting explanation of this. In Yang's community the population was smaller and more stable. With subsistence based in large part on individual landownership, as opposed to tenancy, there was a body of public opinion which could be effectively mobilized on issues of this sort, while in Ch'uhsien such was not the case. Again, whereas in Taitou the farm laborers came most frequently from nearby families and maintained rather close contact with those families, in Ch'uhsien a large number of the laborers came from the outside and the ties with their families were unimportant in the structure of the local community. Farm laborers, however, may not only be strangers but may also be relatives, as in the description offered by Lin Yueh-hwa:

. . . since his nephews were still too young to do all the farm work, Dunglin employed a farm laborer, a man by the name of Nanmin. [Lin has probably chosen a symbolic name here,

---

14 Yang, 1945, pp. 29-30.

though in the absence of the Chinese characters it is impossible to tell for sure. *Nan min* ordinarily means a refugee or a person in bad straits]. He engaged Nanmin to manage the family lands, which he now took back from the sub-tenants ... Nanmin was ... a long-term employee, who was paid in actual money, a wage of forty to fifty dollars per year. He received food and shelter from his master, who also supplied him with farming implements. Nanmin was a man of more than forty years of age; a distant relative of the Hwang family by marriage. The tenuous relationship was enough, however, to make Dunglin call him "uncle," and he was well treated and honored on that account.[15]

The observations I made in Ch'uhsien, a large political and social unit, were not based upon verified statistical techniques and I am not prepared to say what percentage of farmer-laborer relationship included prior relationships based on kinship. It seems significant, however, that none of the several score of farmers who were approached during the study were in any way related to their laborers. On the other hand, the farmer-laborer relationship in Ch'uhsien seemed much more permanent and stable than was reported by Yang for Taitou. In Ch'uhsien a large proportion of the laborers interviewed had worked continually for the same master for periods of five to ten years and more. In these cases the relationships had solidified and contained much affection and the term *kan-ch'ing* was used to describe them. Particularly strong were the ties between the laborer and the small children of the farmer's family. The term 'uncle' was frequently to be heard, despite the total lack of relationship and in the face of obvious status differentials.

---

[15] Lin, 1947, p. 18.

Finally, the long-term worker, though in most instances either an older man who is a bachelor (often the result of continuous poverty since childhood) or a widower, is sometimes a man with a family. When this is the case two alternatives are discovered. The first, and most common, is for the long-term worker to consider his place on the farm in the nature of employment. His own family lives in his native place which is often a long journey away, and he visits or returns to his family only during the slack season. This means that there is a large class of persons engaged in agricultural work who spend the greatest part of their lives away from direct contact with any related individual, spending only a fraction of their time in the bosoms of their families. I shall not pause here to describe further this type of life since a more complete treatment of a similar urban phenomenon, namely, the specific social organizations of the groups of clerks, artisans, and apprentices appears below. The second pattern, displayed by long-term workers who have families, is far less well distributed but deserves comment. It is the phenomenon of the laborer who resides at the farm with his family. In such cases all of the units of his family may be engaged in productive labor which directly benefits the master. Under such an arrangement the wife may work in the fields, particularly when the demands for labor are heaviest as in the season of rice transplanting, while the children tend the buffalo and participate in gleaning and fuel collection.

Though the laborer may develop a close relationship with the master and his family, marked by familiarity in conversation and play, his status remains lower than his host's. Only one case in which a laborer married into his employer's family was recorded by me and in that situation the farmer had no son or logical heir and the laborer married a daughter.

More common than the long-term laborer is the *tuan-kung* who is hired by the day for short periods of time in such labor-demanding seasons as those of planting or harvest. This labor was payed a fixed wage in rice or wheat, the agreement on price being made prior to the commencement of work. Short-term laborers are recruited in various ways. The largest number of the workers in this field are, even in normal years which see no war displacement, transients who live in the north but who follow the crops southward. Many of these workers hope to winter in a city where they try to find employment at such trades as ricksha-pulling and unskilled labor.

A small army of these workers set up crude dwellings of mud and straw just outside the walls of Ch'uhsien, with a concentration near the railroad station beyond East Gate, since they were not permitted to enter the city without passes. After a period of time, however, some of these people infiltrated through the gates and set up their mud huts in the city. Farmers coming to the city visited one of these sections to recruit labor, a pattern which also held for artisans and merchants in the city who needed casual labor.

Even when dealing with transients the farmer tries to get someone on a recommendation rather than trusting to chance. There is a lively fear that the laborer may turn out to be a thief or a bandit and the chances of involving oneself in trouble are reduced if some previous contact has been made. It must therefore be made clear that where possible a farmer prefers to hire individuals who are distantly related to him or have some history of previous contact with some one of his friends or relatives. In this pattern there are faint traces of dependence on kinship, and on the more important elements of institutionalized friendship but, first and last, there is necessarily a large element of first-hand contact with strangers. The farmer, when his *tuan-kung* have been selected, supervises them much more closely than he does his long-term laborers, often working with them to maintain the pace. The temporary workers are given their meals by the farmer, all generally eating together, and they will sleep in the farmer's house. Nearer the city it is customary for the laborers to be given two meals a day and they return to their own huts each night, sometimes with grain or money for their families, the amounts of which are deducted from their wages.

The *tuan-kung* is always on the lookout for an opportunity to improve his lot and seeks to establish favorable *kan-ch'ing* with his employer. A good bond will assure him of work when he comes through the area and, in some cases, may lay the basis for an eventual stroke of fortune— recommendation as a permanent tenant. On the farmer's side, good *kan-ch'ing* means a more reliable source of labor and more efficient work. The war which was raging about Ch'uhsien in 1947-48 created many dislocations in the *tuan-kung* pattern but in the main it retained its features.

When extra labor is required, there are more ways of obtaining it than those given above. The free donation of labor is not usual but in addition to hiring workers there are two major types of labor exchange. The most general system is quite informal and consists of a need on the part of the farmer, his invitation to a nearby relative or friend, and the movement of personnel to his farm for a temporary job. The amount of work which has been put in may or may not be carefully remembered. If the farmer who initiates the request is relatively well-to-do, he is more likely to meet his newly-incurred obligation through extensive feasting or by lending some commodity or labor. Wealthy farmers and wealthy tenants do not always have good *kan-ch'ing* with their poor neighbors. Instead, the popular attitudes towards these people usually obviates the possibilities of labor exchanges involving them.

The labor exchange is an informal cooperative with a fairly stable membership season after season. Each season, however, new arrangements are made in the following manner. A short while before the harvest those farmers who know that they require extra labor to gather their crops, within a reasonable span of time, will find an opportunity to visit those whom they know to be in a position to help. Most of these people have already been involved in such cooperatives. The visit is a pleasant one and may furnish the excuse for some wine drinking. The conversation is mainly about persons known to all and about the farms. Soon the visiting farmer will remark that his own crop should be harvested within a certain period and he will ask when his host's crop will be ready. An agreement, unwritten and informal but as binding as a contract, is made to exchange labor services, the number of units being specified and often including not only the labor of the two men but their wives and children and laborers, if any, as well. The dates of the exchanges are reckoned by the lunar calendar and are specified. The two men then try to enlarge their cooperative to the size deemed necessary by making a number of similar visits to other neighbors and friends. I was interested, during the research on this pattern, in testing the limits of cooperation and in determining the sanctions which controlled and maintained mutual aid of this sort. I therefore invented a number of hypothetical but potential situations in which some type of fraud was perpetrated by a member of the cooperative at the expense of the others. The farmers were much amused at the discussion and admitted that there were ways of manipulating the labor exchanges. They maintained, however, that such activities would be of greatest danger to the manipulator, since, when discovered, he would lose his *kan-ch'ing* and his face.

A sample problem with its 'solution' will illuminate the nature of the labor exchange. A hypothetical statement was made as follows: "If one man was greedy he might always arrange to be first. Therefore he would be protected against the damage of frosts or other natural calamities of weather. He would also profit from the best market conditions when he was ready to sell. Is this not true?" The answer was that such a case was possible but not too likely. The rule in the exchange of labor is that politeness *(k'e-ch'i)* must be observed. Thus, when the question of order in timing arises, the actual process resembles more the classic pose of Alphonse and Gaston than frenzied competition. The violater of this custom would soon be labeled as a person who did not want face *(pu yao lien ti)* and then, since it was a voluntary system, he would find himself unable to get help. Actually, in arranging cooperative work there is not too much leeway for such activity since the pattern covers not only harvests but planting as well, and within the agricultural cycle a more or less natural sequence is established.

The importance of *kan-ch'ing* in recruiting a voluntary

labor party and extending the labor potential of a small farm becomes clearest when observed in crisis. A sudden death or the debilitating illness of a principal in a labor exchange might create such a situation. If the stricken person has a warm bond of affection with his friends and neighbors, the work goes on even though the farmer has no hope of returning the labor. In some cases, death strikes before the contract is agreed upon and the family may be ashamed to ask for labor, knowing that it cannot reciprocate. In such instances, if the *kan-ch'ing* is good, the work parties arrive and work anyhow, though the land of such unfortunates is generally serviced last. The workers in the cooperative parties eat at the expense of the farmer whose land is being operated. In the case of a family in crisis a feast will be served when recovery is made.

Extension of the labor resources of an agricultural family, then, requires an active pattern of relationships which extend beyond those based on some pre-existing tie of kinship. Most agricultural families find themselves at one time or another in the position of requiring more extensive labor and thus the functional importance of extra-kin ties in agricultural production cannot be overstressed.

There is another way in which labor may be multiplied and that is by the use of animals. The addition of animal labor to the farm presents many elements involving basic interpersonal relationships which go well beyond the sphere of kinship. Any farm family which does not have the necessary and available surplus which may be used to buy outright either a water buffalo or a burro may still resort to one of a number of possibilities to gain this valuable labor extension.

The renting of water buffalo, like the hiring of farm

laborers, involves both a long- and short-term possibility. Most common is the long-term rental. Most of the animals available for such rental are owned either by absentee landlords or wealthy peasants and tenants. The rent for the annual use of a water buffalo depends first on the size, sex, and age of the animal and, to a lesser degree, on the *kan-ch'ing* between the contracting parties. As in the collection of land rent, *kan-ch'ing* may be invoked to reduce a rent in time of crisis; it also serves, in a degree, to give some prior claim on the part of the tenant to those animals which are owned by his landlord.

Short-term rental is a system by which animals are let out for a specific task and then returned. Such a system profits not only those who have title to their own animals but also farmers who sublet buffalo which they themselves have acquired on long-term lease. There is a local custom which circumscribes such sub-leasing of animals but this custom may be by-passed either by additional payment to the owner or by having good *kan-ch'ing* with him. The income derived from the sub-letting of a buffalo is very important to farmers whose subsistence is marginal and the *kan-ch'ing* relationship here may be crucial.

Burros are much less expensive than buffalos and rental systems involving them are less frequent. Instead of renting burros, it is more usual to share the animals cooperatively. Even this type of management, however, is more generally applied to water buffalos. The cooperative unit, in the case of animals, is invariably a small village. This village is only occasionally, in Ch'uhsien, a one-name grouping; tenantry, as was explained above, is not conducive to the establishment and perpetuation of villages composed solely of blood related individuals. The number of families in these small villages varies between three and five, on the average, and the purchase price of the animal is shared by all of the household heads. The cooperative ownership of an animal unlike cooperative labor exchange, is quite difficult and represents a constant potential source of conflict. It was explained to me that it is easy to share something made of wood or iron which does not move, eat, or produce young, but the responsibility for and division of an animal involves tricky problems. This attitude, however, does recall the system which is prevalent of sharing a number of tools and implements within the small farming village. Such items include common threshing floors, rice polishing machines, and irrigation pumps. Other, smaller tools are invariably owned by individual families.

One further aspect of the disposition of labor must be treated. This is the problem of dealing with a labor surplus. Such surpluses are of two kinds, a permanent surplus which sees the farmer endowed with a larger family than his land can feed and productively occupy, and a temporary and seasonal surplus which results from the uneven agricultural cycle.

In cases of a temporary surplus of labor, the most usual techniques of amelioration only infrequently involve interpersonal relationships beyond those of kinship. The worker turns his hand to some type of resident handicraft and tries to produce a commodity which combines a readily available raw material, preferably one which requires little or no capital investment, with an accessible market. A less likely alternative sees the farmer enter an urban area during the agricultural slack season and try to earn money there. The latter pattern has two aspects, both dependent on a single element, namely, the status of the family from which the worker comes. At this point, the paramount consideration is kinship and the ties of friendship enter only as secondary forces. To illustrate: the optimum season of cotton ginning and the manufacture of cotton fibre in Ch'uhsien is in winter. Though there are many shops which process cotton the year around, the demand is greatest in winter, when gowns are padded and quilts are in use. Several of the cotton processing shops in Ch'u open only in wintertime when some farmers who have a certain amount of available capital, sufficient to buy the machinery and pay the rent on a store, come to Ch'u and set up in business. To trace one of these stores to its origin reveals a tangle of kin and extra-kin dependences with the emphasis, in this case, on the ties of kinship. A major non-kin relationship is frequently discovered, however, in the arrangement with the landlord from whom the shop is rented. It is not certain in this type of venture that one will be able to return to the same location. The location of any store, however, is not less important in Ch'u than in most commercial places and the proprietor would like to be near the center of town. Here the *kanch'ing* relationship functions again and a landlord will often exert his influence with his friends to get a new place for the farmer turned artisan. The same relationship will often serve as the basis for a favorable credit transaction but this is like similar transactions made generally within the artisan and commercial groups and will be treated below. The temporarily unemployed farmer who does not go into business may perform services for his landlord, for which he will get pay, or at least subsistence, and he will ask the landlord, who is often the only influential contact of the peasant, to place his son or his daughter as a servant.

When it comes to the disposition of permanently surplus farm labor the ties of kinship and the relationships based on friendship and *kan-ch'ing* are at least equally important. At this point, however, I merely wish to note the importance of these relationships in facilitating non-agricultural careers for persons of farm backgrounds. A more detailed treatment of the subsequent effects of such relationships appears below in Chapter V.

Self- sufficiency is rarely possible even for an extended kin group except in such societies as reckon the total population in terms of kinship relationship, as, for example, the tribes of Central Australia. The concept of self-sufficiency is a relative one; to the intensely specialized culture of the urban West, the culture of China, with its tremendous dependence on individual farming, seems to represent almost a peak of family or kin sufficiency. Such a conception, however, quickly breaks down on examination.

TOOLS AND PRODUCTION

It has already been demonstrated that a large proportion of the agricultural population of Ch'uhsien is dependent on non-related individuals for the very land they cultivate. Farmers also rely on non-kin relationships to supply them with the labor they need to cultivate their fields. Still others require outside contacts to relieve themselves of labor surpluses. We shall now carry the analysis one step further and show that the farmer's technology is geared in some measure to an impersonal specialization and that one of the single most important forces in his life, the market, is an entity composed totally of non-kin relationships.

The basic tools with which the soil is cultivated in Ch'uhsien are few and simple. Among other implements there are plows, irrigation pumps, scythes, hoes, stone rollers, and shovels.[16] To make almost any one of these tools requires a special knowledge of materials and techniques, or special access to raw materials. There are some farmers who are capable of manufacturing one or two of their implements but no farmer met by the writer ever was capable of or even wished to make all of them. Instead, tools are purchased from specialists, most of whom are located in the city. This elementary dependence on exchange is possible, of course, only because of the presence of a money economy. The material so far treated was not directly related to this factor, but, once introduced, the very nature of such an economy casts new and welcome light on our inquiry. No one has ever denied the importance of such an economy, but the basic sociological implications of such a system have often been missed or under-rated.[17] The use of money clears the way for immediate interpersonal relationships on a massive scale without benefit of prior meeting, introduction, or kinship. It also encourages the development within agriculture of great specialization, the tendency to produce the cash crop and to

---

[16] For illustrations of these tools see Yang, 1945, pp. 253-255. A more complete guide to Chinese farm technology is R. Hommel, 1937.

[17] A notable example to the contrary is to be found in one recent Chinese study in which the author reports that: "Exchange with town- and city-people is important to the villagers. Non-farm families have to buy their daily necessities either from one of the market towns, or from . . . stores . . . which in turn buy their own provisions from towns and the city. . . . Economic factors have brought the villagers into contact with many strangers, with whom they have to cooperate in order to earn a living." Chao Ch'eng-hsin, 1948, p. 124.

render oneself and one's family dependent on a huge and disorganized mass of unknown individuals who compose the market. In overcoming the difficulties inherent in a system so palpably lacking in personal organization there emerge any number of patterns which are counted upon to bridge the gap of anonymity and the absence of prior claims on loyalty. Many of these techniques are discussed below in the analysis of the workings of a commercial enterprise. We wish to stress here the relationships which are implicit in the assumption by the peasant of the role of merchant, seller of his own produce.

TRADE AND EXCHANGE

To begin with, the peasant or tenant of 1947-48 frequently was spared the necessity of disposing of his surplus by the fact that he had none. Roughly, forty percent of his crop went to his landlord. Another ten or even twenty percent was siphoned off by the direct or indirect demands of the political structure. The Chinese tenant farmer is theoretically not responsible for any taxes, a fact which was frequently cited by the heavily taxed landlords in defense of the high rent.[18] In actuality, however, particularly in the late years of Kuo Min Tang rule, taxes were taken from the tenant, often in the form of voluntary "loans" or "contributions." There is also an almost constant pressure to bribe local officials. The powers of the *pao-chang* for example, included drafting of boys and men for service in the Army.[19] Failure to make a friend of this

------

18 For tax pressures on peasants, see C. M. Chang, 1936.
19 For military requisitions, see Institute of Pacific Relations, 1939, pp. 101-109.

petty officer could lead to calamity. In addition to these drains, all of which induce basic relationships of non-kin nature, the farmer, if he had ever experienced some sort of a crisis, whether natural or social, would be certainly in debt. A large proportion of his gross return from the fields would then flow out in the payment of interest.[20]

Where a surplus remained the farmer would have to estimate and deduct an amount necessary for the subsistence of his family and the seeding of the next crop. He might then be prepared to market the balance. To select a grain-merchant at random was to invite possible disaster. Grain merchants are notoriously talented and can overfill their own containers while they underfill yours. Also, they are superlative talkers and they can bargain you down in a twinkling. It is far better to get someone you know to help you, possibly a relative who has already had such dealings, or a friend, or even the landlord if he lives in town. There is a normal pattern in Ch'u for the tenant to stop at the house of his landlord when he goes to town. There he may rest and get something to eat and a little tea. While he sits he will be told the state of the market and will be advised where and what to sell and where and what to buy. Underlying this relationship, is of course, *kan-ch'ing*. These relationships, if properly conducted, can strengthen the friendship and make future dealings even smoother.

In the preparation of a more general volume descriptive of the culture of Ch'u Hsien, I have had occasion to draw up a diagram which shows the nature of the economic

---

[20] Fei figures all of these categories in his analysis of the distribution of farm expenditures. Fei, 1948, p. 102.

relationships between the various segments that make up
the three main geographic components of Ch'u Hsien; the
city, the countryside, and the outside. Actually no such
word as 'outside' is used in Ch'uhsien in the sense that it
is employed here. When the person of Ch'uhsien mentions
a place that lies beyond the county boundaries, he is likely
to use its proper name, or failing that, the more general
terms is "north part" or "south part," etc. The diagram
is reproduced as Figure 3. Two important facts become
evident from even a superficial inspection of the chart.
First, one notes that the "farmer" group has relationships
with each and every group of specialists who reside in the
city. What is not apparent on the diagram, but which is
even more important, is the fact that almost every farmer
in Ch'uhsien has dealings with all of the population categories in Ch'u. Second, there is a notable difference in
the complexity of relationships between the countryside
and the city and the city and the outside. The effect of
this diagram in creating an impression of the function
of the city as mediator between the countryside and the
outside is quite in keeping with the facts. Though many
farm families maintain connections with kinfolk in the
outside, the basic pattern is maintained and the primary
mediation is still performed by the city.

Operating his farm on the basis of cash crops, the farmer
places the greatest portion of his land into the production
of one or two staple items, the market value of which is
high. The system is quite general in contemporary Chinese
culture. Places as diversely populated and as geographically
separated as the provinces of Fukien,[21] Kiangsu,[22] Kwang-

---

[21] Institute of Pacific Relations, 1939, pp. 122-26.
[22] Fei, 1938; Institute of Pacific Relations, 1939, pp. 73ff.

tung,[23] Hopei,[24] Shantung,[25] and Yunnan,[26] all demonstrate forms of cash cropping involving farm products as different as sheep, opium, and tobacco. In Ch'uhsien there are a number of minor cash crops: tobacco, choice bamboo, certain fruits, and a type of chrysanthemum which is highly prized as a tea flavoring and for medicine (*chu hua*). The main export of Ch'uhsien is grain, particularly rice. Informal estimates indicate that in a good crop year more than fifty percent of the rice harvested in Ch'uhsien is destined for an outside market. A concrete indication of the importance of this trade is the large number of rice agents who descend on Ch'uhsien at harvest time and who try to buy the crops even as they stand in the fields. Such is the value of rice as a means of obtaining cash, that many farmers eat their own rice only at special times of the year. They prefer in many cases to dispose of their entire crop with the exception of seed and invest part of their return in cheaper foodstuffs for their own consumption. Thus many Ch'uhsien rice growers eat maize as their staple.[27] Though a small amount of corn may be raised by a rice farmer, who uses such spare land as the dike ridges for this purpose, the largest amount of maize is produced in the hilly land which flanks Ch'u to the west and south and which is not considered very suitable for rice. Frequently the farmer cultivates no personal garden. Since green vegetables are an important element in the Chinese diet, the farmer who lacks them must get them

---

[23] Kulp, 1925.
[24] Institute of Pacific Relations, 1939, ppfl 160-67.
[25] *Ibid.*, p. 171-175.
[26] Fei and Chang, 1945; Fitzgerald, 1941.
[27] Cf. Institute of Pacific Relations, 1939, p. 93.

through trade or purchase. Under normal conditions of production, therefore, it is quite obvious that the Chinese farm family is far from being self-sufficient. On the contrary the farmer and his family are driven to develop relationships with the outside to insure even their basic subsistence. Furthermore, the network of relationships almost immediately exceeds the geographical and social boundaries of the farmer's neighborhood. Rare indeed is any sort of kin or neighborhood based cooperative which facilitates exchange. Instead, exchange operates in a relatively open market, bound largely by factors of friendship and *kan-ch'ing,* often under the heavy non-kin hand of governmental supervision.

POLITY

The Chinese peasant finds himself in a position which requires the manipulation of many non-kin ties for his economic survival. He is in a similar position with regard to political survival. Where the economic struggle is largely positive, in that the farmer seeks concrete advantages, the political quest is quite negative, the farmer seeking to escape molestation.

The governmental structure of Ch'uhsien was hierarchical, based, at the top, on the county unit or *hsien,* a rural subdivision called the *hsiang,* next in order, with the *pao* or group of households as the succeeding effective political unit and also the simplest active political unit. It is true that ideally the *pao, hsiang,* and *hsien* operated to protect the local peasants from the machinations of the outside. Nevertheless, the prime effect of the political structure in which villagers were actually involved was to function first as a tool of the national power structure.

It collected taxes, implemented labor and military drafts, and maintained a *status quo* in social relationships, especially those involving land tenure. In this last matter, the role of the local rural government in supplying the effective sanction behind the claim of a landlord to his rent was clear, armed soldiers being sent, on occasion, to accessible but refractory areas. Finally, the local authority functioned to protect the people in power from possible depredations from the outside, whether such depredations came through the inroads of beggars and refugees or bandits and thieves.

Especially in such a place as Ch'uhsien, where the one clan village is a relative rarity and tenancy dominated the area, the relationship of the farmer to his local government is singularly free of ties of kinship. In most cases, the farmer is governed by totally unrelated individuals. To maintain good *kan-ch'ing* with these individuals is a paramount need. The poor tenants are precisely the individuals who are unrelated to the officials and who stand most at their mercy, particularly in such a matter as the army draft. There is an institution in Ch'uhsien called *mai chuang ting,* "to buy a body," which theoretically involves a search for a substitute but actually is a bribe to the authorities to pass over the family and look elsewhere. The rich peasants are more likely to be related to the petty local officialdom but even such relationships pale into institutional insignificance when compared with the lack of kinship ties binding them to the urban gentry and officialdom.

RELIGION AND CEREMONIALISM

In the matter of religious and ceremonial affairs, the farmer is more successful in living within a restricted group of kin. The major deities whom he worships are all more or less locally available; that is, there is no great need to visit a specialized temple or house of worship in order to carry on the normal business of life. Most farm houses in Ch'uhsien are associated with small *t'u ti miao*, "temples of the earth god," which are often no larger than three or four feet high by two or three feet across by two or three feet in depth. The *t'u ti miao* contain one, two or three idols representing the earth god, his wife and their son. The *t'u ti miao* are often built and maintained by single families, or by a number of related families, but in Ch'uhsien there are a large number of these tiny temples which have been erected and are maintained by groups of non-related households. The maintenance of the shrine is a common responsibility, decisions to make repairs being made in informal meeting, but the worship at the shrine including the few formal ceremonies of which that of the harvest is most important, is an individual affair.

Certain special conditions, however, cause the religious self-sufficiency of the family to break down and outside resources and specialists are then required. When a woman goes too long without bearing a child, certain steps are in order. In Ch'uhsien, a pilgrimage of sorts was specified. Though the famous and beautiful Lang-ya mountain was convenient to the city of Ch'u it was a long journey by foot (up to three days) for those who lived on the periphery of the *hsien* or even in other nearby counties. The barren woman would repair to the Buddhist temple on Lang-ya mountain and there solicit the help and advice of the clergy. Also very popular were the various temples inside

Ch'u; the temple of the gods of the city and the Taoist temple being most frequented.

During the normal course of a lifetime, however, there are several occasions which require outside help of a magical or religious nature. For a marriage one has to consult a fortune teller and the horoscopes have to be read and compared. For a funeral the services of a geomancer are necessary, if the burial is to be followed by peace for the dead and prosperity for posterity. Even the construction of a house by a rich peasant is the occasion for the specialized work of a geomancer who locates the house properly and safely. Only in the most exceptional cases are the persons concerned able to call upon a relative for the necessary services; in some cases the specialist is a total stranger, in most cases he was an acquaintance or a friend.

Even in some of the most basic aspects of his religious life, the farmer is involved in a process which extends far beyond himself and his family. For most of the ceremonies of the annual calendar there are basic supplies which he requires. Most important of these is incense, the product of an urban specialist. On other festivals fireworks are essential. One needs, if he is poor, a ceramic incense bowl; if he is rich, a pewter one. For funerals a coffin is required and often the land which the geomancer insists is the only possible burial site is the property of a stranger. When the harvest festival comes the tenant visits his landlord and presents him with one or two large baskets of poultry, eggs, vegetables and grain. All of these things he has cultivated himself, but he also tries to show his importance by including one or two special "moon cakes" and perhaps even a can of something made in Shanghai and these things he buys from a local "grocery." Ceremonially, the house is the center of the world, but it is equally true that the home is extremely dependent on the outside world for the proper realization of its desires.

EDUCATION

The farm households, far more than the gentry or the urban commercial classes, maintained their educational system intact and within the home. Formal education for a poor peasant or tenant's son was patently beyond the realm of possibility in the Ch'uhsien of 1947-48, especially if the child lived in the country. It was not that no need for education was felt, since the reverse was actually the case, but the fees for tuition and the expense of boarding a child made the project impossible. In many instances, even the labor of the child could not be spared, a feature reminiscent of some parts of our own country. In a small farm village in Ch'uhsien the child's teachers are all those about him and no more. As we shall see, in the urban areas, formal instruction is quite prevalent. The farm child learns propriety, the techniques of farming, and such sundry specialties as, by good fortune, his parents and neighbors can teach him. In some cases his father will be able to teach him to read enough to decipher the annual almanac with its pithy advice on the procession of days.

Some poor farm children are lucky, however, in that they live in close proximity to a rural school and under certain conditions they may be able to attend the school for short periods of time. In one such school, which was located several miles outside of North Gate, the school teacher had a nucleus of boys of rich peasant origin, all of whom paid for their instruction. A small corps of poor boys were tutored in return for petty services, small and irregular payments, or because they had been recommended by influential families.

The importance of kinship in the educational process cannot, however, be under-rated. Those boys who were most certain of a formal education were the children of richer families. Many poor boys who received educations did so because they were sponsored by their clans. The financial backing was invariably based on family ties and even the teacher was often some relative of the richer boys. Those poorer sons who went to school, however, found themselves tutored by strangers, surrounded by non-related individuals. The rural children, who later passed into the middle school and college systems, found themselves in more impersonal surroundings. Even there, as will be seen below, the effects of kinship were still to be felt. Since this aspect of education is largely an urban phenomenon it is treated in a later section.

RECREATION

The recreational aspects of rural life show a great intensity of relationships based on kinship. For children in a small farm village the number of playmates is restricted and the largest portion of the playgroup always consists of related individuals. There are certain notable exceptions, but these are largely of secondary significance, as, for example, the presence of a long-term laborer who is fond of children and who tells them stories, makes them toys and entertains them when he has leisure. In the matter of recreation the difference between the farm child and the urban child is striking. The farm child lacks the large field of non-kin possibilities which are possible to the city child. The rural child may enjoy the infrequent calls of a wandering toy seller or story-teller, or may have the occasional good fortune to be taken by his parents on a market trip to town, at which time his enjoyment comes from gaping at the sights and costs nothing.

The adults are likewise limited in their recreational possibilities. Most of their pleasures are derived from the observation of the cyclical ceremonials and from the special life crisis rites which involve feasting and celebration. Trips to town for marketing are savored and each transaction while in town is made into a petty ritual. The town merchants understand this and frequently make a small purchase monumental for the peasant by seating him in a chair and offering him tea and a cigarette. Since only the small shops will do this for a person who intends to buy only a small amount, the peasants frequently prefer to trade in the smaller stores. The larger stores, however, draw the more intrepid customers, those who are not too afraid of the sharp tongues of the clerks and who are willing to risk insult to stand in the midst of an imposing array of goods, peer into the back where the wealthy merchant lives, trade jokes and insults with the clerks, and return to the countryside with a fine tale to tell.

non-kin relationships in an
urban milieu

The people of Ch'u, at the time of the study, were engaged in many different and separate professions and employments. These ranged from an indolence very few landlords could afford to such notoriously arduous occupations as smithing and portering. In addition to an increasingly large population of landlords, many of whom had taken refuge within the stout old city walls as the result of a slow but steady growth of banditry, Ch'u had large components of merchants, artisans, laborers, officials, and many gardeners. It is quite true, of course, that most of these people lived in family groups. It is not true that each family represented a world unto itself or even a small republic which, along with several thousand other "republics" maintained a chaste autonomy.

The conditions of life in the city necessitate extensive extra-familial, extra-kin relationship. The city, to a far greater extent than the countryside, sees a breakdown in the importance of the family and of kin ties in the basic orientation of society.

URBAN SPECIALIZATION

To an inexperienced visitor from another culture, such as I was upon my entry to Ch'u Hsien, the old city is a bewildering confusion of people and shops. On the first visit it is hard to say which is more confusing, the crowded streets, which in the Western world are associated with large cities rather than small county seats, or the abundance of shops and streetside merchants. The lines which divide the population of this city into various professions and statuses are quite indistinct. The basketmaker frequently invests some little capital in small articles of trade and combines a handicraft with commerce to increase his livelihood. The wealthy merchant increases or develops his landholdings and often has a larger extent of land than some individual who is a landlord alone. The landlord feels the pinch of reduced means and enters commerce and the clerk renounces the business world and returns to the farm. Under these and similar conditions, precise definition of the various categories of specialization becomes difficult but not impossible. While the areas between the specialties tend to be filled with every conceivable intermediate type, polarities may be distinguished. There are enough landlords whose fundamental income is derived from the collection of rents, enough artisans who spend all of their productive time at their skills, and enough merchants who engage solely in trade to make possible a clear though flexible delineation of specializations in Ch'u. I have selected for separate discussion two major groups. The first group consists of merchants, artisans, and the associated personnel, such as clerks, laborers, and apprentices. These are discussed in the present chapter. The town gentry and officialdom receive separate consideration in a later chapter.

The diversification of the types of merchant enterprises, which operate in Ch'u, reflects the specialization of commerce. The total number of stores in Ch'u in 1947 was 531, exclusive of sidewalk shops and transient peddlers. These shops broke down into 19 separate categories of specialization. The breakdown is not the work of the writer but represents the data of the local commercial guild. It also excludes the large number of handicraft shops which are discussed separately below. The stores range in capitalization from tiny fruit stands, whose total assets do not exceed US $50.00, to large "groceries," whose worth is estimated for tax purposes at well over US $10,-000.00. The shops also range in physical size from the tiny cubby-hole housing the small tea store to the two and a half story building in which one of the great cloth stores is located.

MERCANTILE ENTERPRISES

Three distinct types of financial organization occur in Ch'u: nuclear family enterprises, extended family stores and partnerships. The last category, at a minimum count, includes over 25% of all shops and, as will be seen, applies in the main to the largest shops. All types of organization, however, are found on all levels. The two most popular forms, regardless of size, are family ownership, which in operational actuality might be called the individually owned store, since the head of the family generally operates the store as if it were his alone, and the partnership. Here is one of the first points at which kinship on the functional level in Ch'u seems to break down in favor of a non-kin based organization. The commercial firm, which is owned by an extended famly, does not, except in rare instances operate with maximum efficiency. It is torn with internal strife and the problems which arise are difficult of solution since the major dependence is upon precisely the element which is first to disappear, namely, family unity and a recognition of the prerogatives of the household head. The problem of the extended family in commerce is largely one of maintaining a fine balance, in which the benefits of large scale ownership are played against the drawbacks of conflicting interests, poorly defined rights, and the desire of the individual to protect himself in case of a family split. Opposed to this type of organization is the partnership which is based on contractually stated rights and duties. The partnership stipulates a clear division of the profits, and makes possible a higher degree of efficiency by suppressing certain nepotistic features and better assuring a minimum level of skill for the parties concerned.[1]

Nepotism is one of the major pitfalls in the organization of a commercial enterprise associated with one extended family. The number of collateral relatives who must be given places within an enterprise can often rise to astounding proportions. The obstacles which are placed in the road of commercial development by nepotism are cited by Levy:

Frequently [nepotistic] pressure is so great that a businessman must find sinecures for a host of relatives, friends, or neighbors or face social ostracism. The attempt to use these people in ordinary roles endangers the efficiency of the operation and

---

1 Compare Lin Yueh-hwa, 1947, Chapter XIII.

their sinecures are a great financial burden to the venture. In either case, the modern business role is hindered.[2]

The weight of nepotism was often felt as bitterly by an old style Chinese businessman as by a modern one but techniques existed which made alleviation possible. One way of minimizing nepotistic influences was through the medium of the partnership. By gathering together persons who had small amounts of captital but who were not otherwise related, a group of men of recognized skill and and experience could be recruited as a staff. To facilitate the process, the capital outlay of some "partners" was so small as to be a mere token investment. In a newly activated pottery store in Ch'u, the manager, an experienced man, had made such a token contribution. The rice which he gave was not a fee for the job—it was he who had been first approached. The advance of grain to the business was an instrument by which his appointment could be validated, particularly to certain persons who might feel that their claims to the office had been slighted.

Partnerships may involve persons who are related, a further indication that kin tie alone is insufficient. In such cases the partnerships are designed primarily to increase the amount of capitalization as well as to formalize and contractualize the roles of the various participants in the enterprise. At the same time, use of a civil and legalistic technique of combination permits individuals to escape from the too close and smothering scrutiny of a paternalistic extended family. An example of this kind of partnership may be given from Ch'u. Two young men who were not related pooled their resources and opened

---

[2] Levy and Shih, 1949, p. 2.

a small grain exchange. The staff, which they hired, was largely recruited from persons recommended by friends and relatives and the small shop proved a limited success. A similar story from another part of China, Fukien, is told by Lin Yueh-hwa.:

. . . . Dissatisfied with the allotment of shares (in a family enterprise) that had been given him, Eldest *Go* set to work to persuade Mowhun to be a partner in a new store of their own, free from the control of Dunglin. He stirred up trouble between Dunglin and Mowhun. He demanded that Mowhun withdraw his capital from the store for the new investment. . . .

Finally the two young men found another able young man, by name of Chu Fangyang to join them. Together the three of them decided to start a store dealing in fish and rice after the fashion of the original store of Dunglin's. So the two cousins withdrew their capital from the old store and Fangyang added a share of his own.

In this way a new store came into being. The three partners arranged their work so that Eldest *Go* and Fangyang were actual managers, Mowhun preferring to be nominal supervisor. Fangyang acted at the same time as accountant. They employed some shopmen and apprentices. The new store went successfully enough at the outset.[3]

As Lin details the fortunes of this enterprise, however, there was soon a good deal of trouble. Eldest *Go* discovered fraud in the store accounts and tried to get Mowhun to join him in leaving Fangyang. Though Eldest *Go* and Mowhun were cousins, the wily Fangyang, who was not related to either of them, played upon Mowhun's friendship and won him away. Despite the tie of kin, Eldest *Go* was forced to retire from the partnership. That the

---

3 Lin, 1947, p. 134.

eventual fate of the partnership was total collapse, with the villain, Fangyang, absconding with the funds, paints a familistic moral but does not disturb the fact that in this, as in other instances, ties of kin took a secondary role in the formation of a basic relationship.

The details of the operation of a business firm necessarily involve a great number of ties which have no relation to kinship. To follow, for example, the agent of a large store, as he makes his way out of Ch'u to a source of supply of some specific commodity, is to see a wide network of impersonal relationships revolving about the business of exchange, as well as a good number of more personal ties which aid the businessman but which have nothing to do with kinship. In the case of the pottery shop mentioned above, the original organization deliberately included two men who had prior experience in the field of ceramic buying. These men had little cash to invest but they were invaluable in the actual operation of the store and, even more so, in bringing to the new company a number of previously established ties with pottery manufacturers and jobbers. The biggest investor in the pottery store was a man who had a large general store and he had a fixed agreement with several professional boatmen. Thus, through partnership, there now was a source of supply, capital and a mode of transportation. The actual shop was leased at standard terms from the senior partner and went into operation.

The precise histories of various men of prominence in the commercial world of Ch'u show great variation. Some of the men, like the Alger heroes of American culture, are clearly self-made, starting with nothing and ending in positions of importance and wealth. Stories about such men are current and, though they frequently contain elements which are hardly flattering, the general attitude is that such men are worthy of respect. One of the most notable success stories, told among the merchants in the heart of the city, concerned the people whose store was one of the most modern in town—other than the dentist-photographer shops, this was the only glass fronted store in the city. In 1947, the store was the width of three rooms across its front, but ten years before it had been simply a shallow, one room booth. The explanation given for its growth was that the old store had been selected by the Japanese as a central point for the distribution of opium and that the couple who operated it had flourished on the proceeds of the trade. The details of the opium trade were mentioned without censure; it was said that only the cleverness of the storekeeper's wife had gotten the partial monopoly and the shrewdness of this woman, now dead, was extolled.

When entering commerce, a man will consider his resources, his previous experience and his contacts, both kin and non-kin. On the most moderate financial level the source of original capital frequently proves to be the painstaking accumulation of savings through years of work as a clerk or artisan. Perhaps even more popular, though riskier, is the swift accumulation of capital by smuggling. In China one does not have to live near an international border to enter the profession; it is enough to live near the border of two provinces since there were still, in 1947, several taxes which were collected on the passage of goods across provincial borders. Central Anhwei, however, represented much slimmer pickings then the relatively rich smuggling country of southern Yunnan.[4]

Still considering enterprises of a modest scale, the original capital might come from a friend or relative and be in the nature of a loan. Such is usually the case only when the would-be merchant has already proven himself as some sort of success, perhaps as an itinerant peddlar or *hsiao p'ao*. For one to manage a loan from a bank is a difficulty of prime magnitude unless the borrower is already established. The inflation that raged in China during the period of my study had also made long term loans obsolete and the short term, high interest loan was beyond the capability of the poor man to support, even if he had allied himself with a sufficient number of prominent individuals who were willing to put pressure on the bank on his behalf. The origin of somewhat more ambitious commercial undertakings may sometimes be traced to the proceeds resulting from a division of property. Finally, in the zone of high finance, the income from extensive land holdings may be used to nourish a young business, or the surplus from an established business may be used to start a new one. Actually, the last technique is responsible for the bulk of the capital invested in new and large enterprises.

In each of the previous techniques of initiating a new commercial enterprise, it is quite true, the primary source of capital is either the individual himself or his relatives. In many actual cases, however, ties of friendship or *kan-*

---

[4] See, Fei and Chang, 1945, pp. 280-82. In 1950 Communist authorities estimated that 1.5 million people in Kwangtung engaged in smuggling and that 10,000 persons a day smuggled articles between Hong-Kong and the mainland. N.Y. *Times,* June 4, 1950.

ch'ing are of first rate importance. This is true of business men of all degree of wealth. One Ch'u man was a merchant in a small way, selling dried fish and dried and pickled vegetables. He had been trained as a geomancer but his youth counted against his extensive employment. Nevertheless, he had managed to save some money. His basic capital consisted of this amount plus a substantial loan at a favorable rate of interest. This had been advanced by a young landlord with whom the young geomancer had managed to establish excellent *kan-ch'ing*. The way in which the two men built up their friendship is interesting. They had first been introduced when the landlord was seeking a suitable burial place for his mother. The two made several walking trips through the countryside and discovered mutual interests. The geomancer's father, a merchant, had managed to send his son through a few years of middle school before his business collapsed, and so the geomancer and the landlord met on compatible ground. The friendship had no base in kinship and eventually was used by the geomancer to help establish his own business.

Another way in which a business enterprise might be begun also utilized a tie that was not kin based. Among the various commercial roles in Ch'u there is one called *ch'u shui yuan,* a person who operates between Ch'u and Nanking, taking orders from small and large firms for merchandise from Nanking and delivering the goods, bringing reports on market conditions, and making occasional sales of Ch'u commodities in Nanking. Most of the large stores use one of their favored clerks as a *ch'u shui yuan* but will, on occasion, employ an independent professional. In one instance observed in Ch'u Hsien, such a professional, having made a success at travelling, but wishing to settle down and open a small store dealing in imported goods, *e.g.*, thermos bottles, plastic combs, ready made clothing, and cosmetics, managed to do so with the money he had saved and the active support of a large merchant for whom he had done commissions.

COMMERCIAL GUILD

The 531 shops that were open for business in Ch'u Hsien in 1947 were effectively joined together in a merchant guild. The present guild actually has been in formal operation only since 1945 when, after the defeat of the Japanese, a political officer of the KMT was sent from Nanking to establish a new guild to supercede the old informal one which had operated throughout the war, and which had held Japanese sanction.[5] The official aims of the guild, as presented in the guild charter, are three: first, to improve and stimulate trade between Ch'u Hsien and the outside; second, to improve the general standard of living through increasing the amount of goods and by standardizing and improving the quality of goods; third, to improve and standardize local business methods.[6] The present guild is a creation of the outside, but it operates over ground similar to that covered by guilds in Ch'u for decades. The hand of the Nationalist government in the guild of 1947 was, however, heavy and obvious. The guild could suspend its functioning only with the permission of the National Government. It might be suspended and de-

---

[5] Compare the role of the government in establishing the Butcher's Guild in Hsichou, Yunnan. Francis L. K. Hsu and J. H. Hu, 1945, p. 357.
[6] Compare functions of Peking Guilds as given by Burgess, 1928, pp. 190-200.

prived of function by the government for illegal or unpa-
triotic activities. Individual members might leave the
guild only to move or to close shop and even then the
prior permission of the guild had to be granted. Any member whose conduct was considered hostile to the Government, including persons who embezzled government funds,
criminals and those convicted of crimes, persons in bank-
ruptcy, notoriously inefficient businessmen, and opium
smokers, all of these were to be dealt with by the guild and
punished according to the severity of the offense.[7] The
punishments meted out by the guild were not a substitute
for but in addition to any punishments that might be imposed in the regular courts of law. The four grades of
punishment of the guild were: (1) warning, (2) fine, (3)
suspension, (4) permanent ouster with resultant theoretical ostracism. The action was to be taken by the council
of delegates and the vote needed was a plurality.[8]

The importance of the guild cannot be magnified. It
is not possible to do business in Ch'u unless you are a
member. However, anyone who has the necessary capital
to open a store, and who can find a place to do business,
if he is able to get supplies, may join the guild. No merchant could recall an instance, since the reformation of the
guild, of a shop being forbidden to open or ordered by the
guild to close. Thus the guild of the post-war period was
not used as an instrument of monopoly control or field
limitation. Such abuses, however, were said to have occurred before the war. When merchants were asked to

---

[7] Note the much less stringent government control of the Peking Guilds
in 1926-27, *Ibid.*, pp. 31-36, 227-233.
[8] Compare Burgess, 1928, pp. 200-208.

explain the shift, the difference in the functioning of the guild was laid to the general contraction in Chinese economy which had in other ways controlled the number of competing shops.

The guild has no formal credit function.[9] Each member must arrange and deal with his credit problems individually. The guild is theoretically supposed to report instances of usury to the government for official control but, since the merchants are either the usurers or are linked to the usurers through kinship or *kan-ch'ing*, this function has probably never operated. The guild does, however, keep a weather eye on credit facilities, and information and advice are exchanged among the members. The guild hierarchy was well connected with the heads of the three foremost local banks, the Bank of China, the Anhwei Provincial Bank, and the Ch'u Hsien County Bank. The credit facilities of these banks, which were limited to 25% interest monthly, a startlingly low figure in view of the inflation, were virtually monopolized by a few important persons. The guild is capable of taking up a collection upon the death of a member but all contributions are voluntary. For a poor member, the donation will be in money; for a wealthy one, the donation consists of funeral scrolls or a plaque celebrating the deceased.

The guild has no precise and formal role in the collection of taxes, as far as the government is concerned, but one of the guild's most important functions is involved in the tax problem. Each merchant is supposed to deal

---

[9] The basic works in English on the subject of guilds would seem, at least by omission, to be in accord. One source mentions mutual help such as charity, or death-benefits but does not speak of credit. Tsu Yu-yue, 1912, pp. 89-92.

directly with the tax bureau of the local government. Actually he relies to a large extent on the guild for information about his tax status. Also, in the last months that Ch'u operated under the Nationalist Government, the taxes multiplied and many were not of the official type. The normal list of taxes included income tax on merchants (*so te shui*), stamp tax on receipted transactions (*yin hua shui*), individual family tax (*hsin ch'in pao shih*), profit tax (*li te shui*), provincial sales tax (*yin yeh shui*), provincial self defense corps tax (*tzu hui tui chun shui*), license tax (*p'ai chiao shui*), and such local taxes as repair streets tax (*kung lu fei*), among others. There was also a new and special list of military demands including such levies as *fu tzu fei* which was a demand for labor or its equivalent to transport army supplies, *chuang ting chun* which was a heavy tax on conscriptable civilian males, and two further and notorious levies which almost drove Ch'u Hsien to separate rebellion, *tan p'ai shui* and *ma ts'ao ma liao*, the first being a demand for "furniture" for army use and the second, fodder for animals and soldiers. The last two were delegated specifically to the guild for collection. Much friction resulted, since the poorer merchants claimed that they were paying an undue share.

To say that the tax burden on all grades of merchants was huge is to be redundant in view of the partial list above. The guild stood as a prime mediator in the process and continually led the drive for lower taxation. There were three ways to solicit tax relief in Ch'u. The best was through kinship affiliation, to be related to a prominent official or high military person who would intercede for you. The second best method was to be friendly with such a person of influence or to have a solid tie of *kan-ch'ing* with him. Least satisfactory was to protest as a group. The guild, though most effective, was only occasionally and partially successful. The guild also reported local business conditions to the government and supplied details on capitalization for tax purposes. Much of this information was fraudulent and a good deal of collusion was involved in the preparation of these statements. Internal manoevering in the guild for the purpose of reducing tax obligations was extreme. Though not at point in the present paper, it was one further element in the Chinese economic structure of 1946-48 that probably speeded the eventual military collapse of the KMT government. In dealing with the special demands of the army the guild eventually set up a special sub-group called the *chun min ho ts'o pu,* the "cooperate-with-the-army office."

The main function of the guild in Ch'u was to regulate the price structure. To this end the guild directed each subguild to issue periodical price lists which were to be displayed publicly and to which adherence was demanded. The sanction involved was, however, only partly the responsibility of the guild. The major sanction was a legal one. The county government posted occasional copies of the guild lists and asked the general public to cooperate in maintaining the price levels, threatening violators with arrest and imprisonment. During my residence in Ch'u no such penalty was meted out to any established merchant despite frequent violations. An old technique of control was used, however, on a few occasions. On one holiday a baker was discovered selling short weighted ceremonial cakes. Several of his cakes were nailed to posts around the city and the name of the store and its manager were displayed. The man lost his entire investment in cakes and suffered a great loss in prestige. In other instances, the wrath of the law was felt by peddlers. One old woman was paraded through the streets by the town crier who beat his gong and shouted, "Look at this profiteer who sells much needed bean curd at huge profits!" Other peddlers had their scales seized or their goods impounded.[10]

The Ch'u guild has formal connections with guilds in other places. The most important ties are with guilds in Nanking. Some benefit is derived by the merchants of Ch'u from the limited exchange of price and commodity information which takes place. The merchant who is looking for a scarce commodity may be helped by the guild system but this is hardly likely, unless, in addition to his guild membership, he has ties of kinship, friendship or *kan-ch'ing* with persons in the other guilds or he works through an intermediary.

The internal structure of the Ch'u Merchant Guild in no wise resembles the organization of a family, and, though we have not gone into detail on the matter, it does not show any marked resemblance to the formal political structure of a *tsu* or clan.[11] A few facts concerning guild organization are particularly relevant. First, the guild has two leaders. The nominal head is not himself a merchant but is a local gentleman of accepted prestige and high status. The older is an informal leader who is always a prominent merchant of great wealth. The leadership of the guild, whether formal, as in the case of the gentleman, or practical, as in the case of the powerful merchant, is

---

10 See, Fried, 1949, p. 123.   11 Compare Hu, 1948, pp. 20-22.

allied to the general membership through ties of mutual interest. The precise interpersonal relationships are cemented individually on the basis of friendships and *kan-ch'ing*. The membership of the merchant guild includes many persons whose native place is not Ch'uhsien. Some members are not even from Anhwei province. Ch'u persons, however, compose the majority; the second largest group comes from Chinkiang, Kiangsu.

The guild has three active offices, one dealing with formal guild affairs, such as price and trade practice fixing, and one dealing with human affairs. This last bureau was important as a link between the workers and the shop owners. During 1948 this bureau negotiated with representatives of the clerks who sought higher wages in the face of growing inflation. The fact that the clerks attempted to bargain collectively rather than as individuals or shop by shop has some significance. The normal relationships between master and employee within the shop are based on nepotism and *kan-ch'ing*. In a system of collective bargaining the operating principles are even more abstract and kin-removed.

The third office of the guild was for accounting. The strategic importance of the accountant lay in his function of assigning special tax shares and of ultimate responsibility for the maintenance of price control.[12]

The Chinese merchant does not operate in a context of familial relationships, he moves in a world of objective and often impersonal contacts. He regulates his business,

---

[12] Compare Morse, 1909, p. 18, ". . . .monthly account sales are sent in to the (Shanghai Tea) gild, and the penalty for understatements discovered by the gild audit is a fine of fifteen times the difference . . ."

not according to the needs and demands of his relatives, but according to the stipulations of a largely external social structure. While it is true that at many points the merchant makes concessions to his kin, particularly by employing relatives in his enterprise and helping them on the way to individual success, nevertheless, the major portion of his behavior follows rules established and controlled by non-kin demands. Since the good fortune of the merchant rests, in part, on the cultivation of the guild authorities, a substantial portion of the businessman's time is occupied in establishing and cementing friendships with persons of influence in commercial and guild circles. This is paralleled by the necessity of enlisting as friends the various bureaucrats whom he may contact. The best way of insuring good relationships with the government is to be represented in the official hierarchy by a relative. Obviously this technique can work to advantage only in a few case, the majority must devise other ways of solving the problem. Possible solutions call for the cultivation of friendships or the development of *kan-ch'ing*. As in the case of a merchant wooing the powerful members of the guild, dinners are served, invitations are freely passed, and gifts and favors are granted. Sometimes, of course, bribery is the resort, but graft rarely passes in an abrupt or direct manner, instead, the passage of a bribe will simply be one element in a lengthy and complicated transaction.

CLERKS

The established merchants live with their own nuclear families and spend a good deal of time in contact with individuals who are related to them by blood. The big

merchant is rarely separated from his family for long periods of time. He may take occasional trips to explore business possibilities or to call upon the important representative of certain key firms with which he deals, but he is
accustomed to living at home. This is not the case with
many of the clerks who work in the merchant shops.

Clerks are diversely recruited. Most of them owe their
positions in the enterprise either to kinship or friendship
with the owner. Kinship, by itself, is often insufficient.
Merely to be able to establish a remote degree of relationship with the *laopan* does not necessarily insure a position,
nor is it assurance that the position, once granted, will be
maintained. Within the distant degrees of relationships
kan-ch'ing begins to operate, as effectively as in the case
of a tenant farmer and his landlord.

The organization of one of the great "grocery" stores in
Ch'u is worthy of treatment as an example of the complexity of mercantile enterprises. The number of persons employed varied through the years because of illness, termina-
tion of apprenticeship, and the oscillations of trade. On
the average, this shop employed some 32 workers in its
main store. Of this number only one-third were even distantly related to the *laopan*. More than two-thirds, however, came from the *laopan's* home district in Kiangsu.
Others came from such diverse localities as Ch'uhsien,
Shanghai, and a number of tiny villages in counties near
Ch'uhsien.

Acquaintance with an influential intermediary was
often far more important than kinship in obtaining employment, but relationship, too, was of importance. A close
tie, such as that between brothers or uncles and nephews,
could often suffice, in and of itself. More distant kin ties,

however, such as those between cousins, matrilineal or conjugal relatives, or affinal relatives who lived far off, were generally insufficient without other reinforcement. A tie based purely on friendship or *kan-ch'ing* might work in these areas, when kinship alone would be inadequate. A recommendation from the *laopan* of the store in which I lived was acted upon almost as a directive. After completing apprenticeships in this store, several young men were swiftly assigned to similar stores through the offices of the *laopan*. These men were not related to the *laopan* but had come to him with recommendations of their own. One had come from Kiangsu with the endorsement of the family branch there, two others came from the Ch'uhsien hinterland, bearing the compliments of a prominent Ch'uhsien landlord and politician. Even one young clerk, whose performance dissatisfied the *laopan* and who was discharged at the New Year, was given a valuable boost by the master when he was directed to the wheat flour mill outside of East Gate and there was sold bags of flour at a reasonable price for resale. The *laopan* was unwilling to recommend this clerk further, but he did help him begin his own small business.

The majority of the clerks, even those whose original homes are in villages not far from Ch'u do not see their families more than once or twice a year. For great periods of time they live in a world that is circumscribed by the store and by their commercial duties. In the store whose organization we are considering, a total of 25 out of 32 workers lived in the shop, only seven men returning to their homes in Ch'u each evening. For the 25 who stayed there were several sleeping places. In one room, the bakery, were housed the bakers, candle makers, condiment makers and one or two of the clerks. Some laborers and apprentices slept in a rickety second story room over the rear of the house. This room, the dimensions of which are approximately 25 feet by 20 feet, was reached by a ladder. It contained some dozen beds, each consisting of two saw horses and three boards, a straw matting and blankets. (In summer only a thin straw mat topped the boards.) Under some beds there were chests for the storage of personal goods, but most of the clerks were unwilling to spend money on a chest and preferred to make a bundle of their possessions. The whole room was illuminated at night by two of the cheapest and smallest kerosene lamps available.

The clerks worked a day of variable length. In summer they rose at six and the store, open at seven, remained open until about eleven at night. In winter the store opened about eight and closed about six. There is very little leisure time which a clerk may utilize for himself. Most of the day he is occupied at the counter; if idle, he may not leave the store. He spends the day in conversation with his fellows or he reads novels or illustrated stories. He takes his meals with his companions, eating directly behind the counter, and often has to jump up to serve a customer. At night he retires to the barrack-like room and there he may try to sleep, gamble, mend his clothes, read or write a letter home. The author lived in the room described above for about three months and had no difficulty in adjusting to it, since it seemed nothing so much as a continuation of barracks life in the Army.

There are often several clerks who are distantly related to each other. This is sometimes an advantage in the early establishment of friendships. Often such kin ties are overridden by prolonged contacts which involve only personal reciprocation and have no context of kinship. For the most part, however, the clerks form shifting cliques which operate in a small circle of non-kin relationships. Except for a brief annual reunion with their families, the clerks confine their activities to the shop which is the scene of friendly devotion, open animosity and at least a little homosexual play. The most important person on the social horizon of a clerk is his *laopan*. Frequently the first meeting between the two occurs when the clerk comes as a boy to be an apprentice.[13] In some cases, however, the clerk is first employed as an adult. The *laopan* is sometimes a more or less distant relative. Several clerks in the store which we have described were related to the *laopan* through marriage. More often the *laopan* is only the friend of a friend.

Within the store, the word of the *laopan* is law. He frequently gives direct commands to the clerks and the apprentices are always being ordered about. The tension in the shop is always greatest when the master is present and in bad humor. When the *laopan* is out for the day or away on a trip the air is noticeably less strained. However, not all of the relationships between the clerks and their master are of an unpleasant nature. Particularly at festival times the atmosphere becomes light and more permissive as the master treats his staff to an enjoyable few days. Most notable are such holidays as the eighth month festival

---

13 This practice is thought a wise one since it is conducive to discipline. By extension, "the practice of exchanging sons for training is considered a wise step, for each father is afraid of spoiling his own son if under his own care. Practices of this kind are found more often in the North." Liao T'ai-ch'u, 1948, p. 93 note 2. Such an institution, which does not seem to appear in Ch'u, further extends the importance of non-kin relationships among the merchants.

when the store is closed early and the clerks are given money to go to a local bath house and relax. Even more important is the New Year holiday which sees the shop closed for three or four days during which the clerks are free to amuse themselves as they see fit. On the first night of the New Year holiday it is customary in Ch'u for the head of a firm to entertain his staff. A large feast is prepared, which all enjoy, and the master plays various gambling games with the most important clerks and artisans. If he wins, he distributes all of his winnings to the clerks who cluster about him; he also encourages the clerks to eat, gamble and make merry, drinking wine with them during the meals or putting up a representative to drink for him.

Actually, there is a hierarchy of small positions within the store. The roles, in the order of importance, are clerk, shopman and apprentice.[14] The apprentice combines the work of a junior shopman, general roustabout and servant. He is not addressed by name but responds to call *"Shuang-a!"* by all above him, including the shopmen and clerks.[14a] A boy serves as apprentice for a minimum of three years, during which time he does one or another of the tasks in the store, from waiting on customers to reckoning the accounts. He also does most of the menial household labor, waking up earliest in the morning to help the cook with the fire and retiring last at night after closing the front of the shop.[15] During the first week of my

---

[14] Compare Liao T'ai-ch'u, 1948, p. 94.

[14a] I failed to procure the Chinese characters for this expression but believe it may be translated as a command, "Come quickly!" The person of lowest status who is within earshot then comes forward.

[15] Liao gives a graphic description of the rough lot of an apprentice which may lead to suicide. *Ibid.*, pp. 94-97.

residence in Ch'u, an apprentice of the shop at which I lived was ordered to sleep on the floor next to my bed to make certain that any nocturnal emergency could be met. For all of this service the apprentice gets no formal pay. He receives his board and lodging and a small amount of money each month, the money being used to pay for his laundry, bathing, and small needs, such as cosmetics. The apprentice may return home, like the clerks and shopmen, once or twice every year.[16] Few apprentices do so for lack of money. When an apprentice who lives far away goes home it is believed that he will not return, so customary is it for him to remain his full term before departing.

At the end of three years the apprentice may continue as a shopman, providing that he satisfies certain conditions. He must have proven himself a good and intelligent worker, there must be a possibility of using his services, and the relationship which got him his apprenticeship, whether kin or non-kin, must still be operative. If these conditions do not hold, there are various possibilities. If he proves a poor worker or if his *kan-ch'ing* is defective, he must return to his home or take his own chances in the town for the *laopan* will not give him a recommendation. If his *kan-ch'ing* is good and he has some ability, his future as a shopman is more secure for, in addition to employment in the original shop, he may be recommended anywhere that his *laopan* has effective influence. Even should a man elect to return home after apprenticeship, as was the case of one apprentice known to me whose parents needed his labor on their small farm near Chinkiang, he has a valuable skill that may be used

---

16 Liao states that there are no vacations for apprentices. *Ibid.,* p. 97.

to advantage during the farm slack season.[17] The month or two before the New Year holiday is a time of great buying in China. The town streets are crowded with peasants and even the townspeople begin to amass holiday stores. The shops, during this period, are pressed for help and experienced personnel is much in demand. During this period, the store in which I lived hired two shopmen who lived in Ch'u. Of the two, one bore only routine recommendations from a tiny shop outside East Gate, and the other was a merchant whose own small store had finally gone bankrupt. The first man worked the holiday season and was discharged, the second man was added to the permanent staff.

The position of shopman is intermediate between the apprentice and the clerk but may prove to be a permanent rank since the jump to clerk depends more on the nature of one's contacts than on the work which he does. The incidence of nepotism increases sharply as one ascends the ladder of shop ranks. The shopman devoted his major energies to servicing the shop counter but he may also be employed at such tasks as making minor trips to the bank. (When the inflation grew to record proportions, the shopman would take an apprentice with him just to carry the basket of money.) He might also make short trips to Nanking or nearby county seats to check on prices and supplies. The shopman received his board and lodging and also a monthly wage which during my residence fluctu-

---

[17] Apprenticeship does not mean automatic acquisition of a valuable skill. "An earnest apprentice would either have to *t'ou shih,* meaning to steal the technique by unhealthy channels, or to cultivate friendship with the (master) and by affirming his undying faithfulness and loyalty to him hope that he may be given a chance to learn all the secrets." *Ibid.,* p. 96.

ated between the equivalents of US$2.—and US$6.—depending on the exchange.

The clerk is a skilled shopman who is adept at figures and accounts and who may be entrusted with the control of a section, especially in the absence of the *laopan* or the small *laopan*. Most clerks are middle aged or older but some favorites of the *laopan* advance rapidly and become clerks before they reach thirty. Unlike the shopmen, who are simply called by name, the clerks are called by name and the title "Mister" (*hsiensheng*); the apprentices and the shopmen always call the clerks *hsiensheng*.

Each of the three groups tends to form an independent social group, but the apprentices, after a short while, begin to mingle with the younger shopmen. Friendships are largely found within status levels. When they cross-cut status lines they prove of great benefit to the junior man. Such friendships are actively cultivated by the younger men. Many small favors and services will be performed in order to gain the good graces of an established individual such as the accountant or a little *laopan*.

Most relationships between clerks and customers are of a transient nature and do not exceed the limited over-the-counter contact. Within this type of relationship there are three notable sub-patterns. In the large shops the peasant customer is at a disadvantage. His patronage is not generally solicited except by the smallest merchants. In a big store he is expected to order quickly and pay without argument. One major difference between the big "grocery" stores and most of the other types of stores is the grocery's fixed price policy. Many stores of all types in Ch'u boast large signs that proclaim them 'one-price' stores but, invariably, they too permit bargaining. Such is not the custom in the "grocery" shops and the peasants, who are accustomed to haggling over prices, only are insulted by the clerks for their attempts. Frequently, the clerks will call to one another that one or another peasant is a 'turnip head', a local term of derision. During a transaction with a peasant the clerk will drop the merchandise on the counter and, when making change, he literally throws the money at his customer. When dealing with an established member of the gentry, a well-dressed stranger, or a soldier, the transaction is quick and polite. Pains will be taken to give good merchandise and complaints about prices will be met sympathetically. Often in this category of customers are personal friends of the *laopan* or of the clerks. These people are offered stools, cigarettes, and tea. Sometimes they are engaged in extended conversations. Sometimes gifts are placed with the purchases over the polite objections of the customer. It was this group of patrons that did most of the credit buying before the inflation curtailed such transactions. Even in 1948 a certain minimum of credit buying persisted, but even this had changed and was now recorded in terms of rice rather than as currency. Certain influential persons such as military officers still were granted credit at the old terms but this was a recognized way of buying good will which elicited private complaints and curses from many a *laopan*. The third type of dealing was infrequent since it involved a face to face transaction between the merchant and a customer of truly high status such as a magistrate, a secretary of the county government, a high military officer, or a truly prominent local citizen. In such cases not even a clerk waited upon the customer but one of the little *laopan* served the personnage. In most cases the official, who generally arrived in a ricksha, an unheard of thing in the small city, was invited into the laopan's "office" (the family shrine) and had his needs filled while discussing events with his host. Such customers would be invited to take a meal but invariably refused, though they occasionally attended more formal banquets in the same house. This type of contact was rare, however, since high status individuals invariably sent servants to do their shopping. One exception, the magistrate of a neighboring *hsien,* had the unflattering local reputation of being slightly insane.

ARTISANS

The people engaged in handicrafts in Ch'u recognize themselves as distinct from the merchants who were described above. The primary evidence of this dichotomy is the separation of the merchant enterprises from the handicraft and service enterprises. The two distinct guilds which result are capable only on exceptionally rare occasions of cooperative measures. The types of industries and services which made up the local service guild may be found in the Appendix.

In most instances, the crafts are conducted in small shops which are similar in some ways to the least impressive merchant enterprises. The buildings are of mud and thatch but lack counters. The entire front room is open and used as a workshop; supplies are stored in the rear. The goods, when completed, are displayed in front of the store and if a person stops to look at them the worker immediately engages him in conversation. The craftsmen sell their own production every day but there are seasons when trade is heavy and periods when hardly anyone buys.

If the craftsman is poor, but has tiny surplus, he is likely to buy small commodities such as candy, toys, or fruit and sell these things as well. No special person in the store is specifically charged with the making of sales. Though the master is likely to do more selling than anyone else, even an apprentice is supposed to know the value of the products and be able to make a sale. If the master of the store becomes wealthy he is likely to cease his productive activities and content himself with supervision of the work and the sales.

A more detailed description of the actual working of two diverse crafts will give a background from which we may draw effective generalizations. Basketmaking is one of Ch'u's largest crafts, having some 105 shops and employing the services of about 550 people. Half of this force is composed of adults, mostly males, and the balance consists of apprentices and to a greater extent, the employed children of basketmakers. The center of the basketry trade is near the East Gate, because two of the three major markets are connected with the outside. One is the export of baskets to Nanking and the other is the sale of baskets to travellers on the railroad. Ch'u has a reputation of producing some of the best baskets in central China and travellers like to buy this specialty. (Almost every Chinese city is noted for something and the traveller is expected to avail himself of the opportunity to sample these things. Thus, when I told my friends in Ch'u that I was making a trip to Honan, I was advised to buy wine in Hsuchow, pears in Tangshan, and eat a certain pork dish if I got to Yangchow.) There are also smaller centers of basket production at other gates where the basket makers say they pay less for bamboo because they are a bit closer to the source of supply. Basketmaking is the least specialized of all the Ch'u crafts and when one asks how the skill is acquired, the answer is the same as in Yunnan, "Learn by looking."[18] The equipment necessary is also small and as a result many farmers employ themselves at basketry during the slack season.

The making of baskets may be divided into two major tasks, the splitting and preparation of the bamboo and the actual weaving. When the artisan employs an apprentice or a young child, the boy will do all of the splitting and the more experienced hand will turn out the basket. A large variety of basket types is manufactured and the saying "learn by looking" does not do justice to the skill of the master basket maker. Discounting the price of the raw material, which is negligible, the price of a basket represents little more than subsistence for the labor involved [19] and sometimes barely enables the craftsman to make a living since the competition is keen and the market is limited.

Apprenticeship in the basket shop shows many features that typify the general conditions of the artisan apprenticeship. The apprentice basket-maker serves for a three year period and gets no formal wage. Instead, he is given lodging of a rough sort, three poor meals a day, and two sets of clothing a year, one winter and one summer. This clothing is itself quite poor and consists of the painfully restitched castoffs of an older person. Unlike the merchant's apprentice, the basketry apprentice rarely gets even a tiny amount of spending money and is notoriously unkempt

---

[18] Compare Fei and Chang, 1945, p. 174.
[19] *Ibid.,* pp. 173-176.

and thin. Under these conditions, how does a boy become such an apprentice and why does the master take him in?

The latter point is simpler. The master gets the profit of the boy's labor. By setting the apprentice the task of bamboo preparation he extends his time and labor power. Since the cost of lodging is nil and the food is meager he welcomes apprentices to the limit of his ability to buy bamboo and put up the boys. On the side of the apprentices the reasoning is different. Most of these apprentices are country lads. They are the youngest sons in households which are pressing their land too closely. Not only is there no productive work which they can do with any economic value, but the subsistence level of the household demands that they leave so that the productive workers may be properly fed. The mere feeding and lodging of the boy will take some weight off the household, at least temporarily; then, through death or some other circumstance, when the farm balance improves, the boy can return. Frequently he does not return but opens his own shop or drifts into some other employment.

There is also a group of journeymen basketmakers. These individuals are those who have passed through their apprenticeship but who have not even the tiny capital necessary to rent a place to work and buy a load of bamboo. Such men attach themselves to a master basketmaker and work on a piece-rate basis, receiving about 25% of the price of each basket for themselves. In addition to this wage, the basketmaker gets two spare meals each day, frequently wheat or maize rather than rice. His position is miserable, which he himself remarks. He is also likely to shrug his shoulder and say bitterly, *"Mei pan-fa,* (no way out)."

The *laopan* of some basket stores live in comfortable circumstances. One man, who had the largest basket shop in Ch'u, housed his enterprise in five rooms for which he paid a substantial monthly rental. He had six apprentices and also hired six journeymen. This man never touched the bamboo himself but was content to supervise the shop and sales. His main occupation seemed to be the extensive conversations he held with one and all, including some men who never worked and who were believed to be the center of such smuggling and illicit trade as went on in Ch'u Hsien. It was said that this man, who himself had been only a poor basketmaker in his youth, had made his money smuggling opium and other "troubles" into Nanking. Though it was usual for the head of the small shop to eat with his employees, this man never did so but always ate apart with friends or with members of the gang. He was also notable among basketmakers in that his children did not work, being quite young, but he planned to send them to school and hoped to set them up as merchants when they got older.

Basketmaking is a typical small handicraft industry and some of its problems and symptoms are representative of all small handicraft enterprise. The basketmaker is dependent for his supply of raw material on persons with whom his only relationship is through trade. In his dealings with farmers he tries to build up some *kan-ch'ing* in order to insure a supply of good bamboo even in bad years; he also tries in this way to minimize the bad effects of competition for the best bamboo. In his shop, the craftsman depends only to a limited extent on his own labor. For the most part, particularly in the case of a man who is successful to some degree, he utilizes the labor of others, generally strangers. His relationship with these persons are based primarily on the conditions of the trade. No attempt, beyond the most simple generalities which flow from common residence and prolonged personal contact, is made to equate the functional handicraft household to a family, either in structure or in operation. Finally, the disposal of the product takes place through a series of impersonal trade relationships which have no analogies to patterns of behavior associated with kinship.

A second specialty, which will give opportunity to augment the observations already made is that of tinsmith (*t'ung-chang*). This is a much less popular industry than basketmaking. It has about 10 shops employing some 20 persons. Most of these shops are in the center of the city. This ecological factor is of some concern. Each industry tends to have a specific distribution of shops. The factors involved in the concentration or dispersal of shops include such things as availability of raw materials, the location of markets, and the level of rents. Since these factors, which are of a distinctly non-kin and industrial nature, take precedence over such other factors as the desirability of locating near relatives or the continued occupation of a traditional family location, the inference about the relative weight of kin and non-kin forces is clear.

To open a tinsmithy requires much more capital than does a basket shop though the absolute amount is still small. The tools required include mallets, hammers, heavy shears, and a supply of materials including raw materials which are not produced by the tinsmith but must be bought by him from the outside, thus necessitating a contact which is invariably of a non-kin trade nature. The products of the tinsmith are many; his best sellers are pails, kettles and small lamps. He is also the recognized source of supply for piping, tin sheeting and special metal containers. He also manufactures and sells the religious candelebra found in homes of the well-to-do, a favorite wedding gift for those who can afford it. Additional money is made from repairs on all the above, but there is great competition, since there are many itinerant tinkers who carry their shops on their shoulders and who will accept much smaller fees. The tinsmith who manages to accumulate surplus capital seeks new fields for investment. One of the most popular is the purchase of large kerosene pressure lamps which are rented for weddings, funerals and celebrations.

Like the basketmaker, the tinsmith has apprentices and may employ journeymen. This is a good trade to learn and in the selection of apprentices the tinsmith resembles the merchant more than the basketmaker. Whereas the basketmaker could often go so far as to take in an apprentice after casual bargaining with a self-introduced peasant, the tinsmith saved his apprenticeships for relatives, friends, and the persons recommended to him by persons he respected or to whom he was obligated.

The foremost tinsmith in Ch'u managed, largely through shrewd commercial manoevering and hard work, to accumulate a fair surplus. After enlarging his enterprise to the extent of subsidizing two of his former apprentices and opening a branch shop, he speculated in land and bought over 100 mow which he rents to tenants. He himself does not do any more hand work, though he will sit down from time to time and make something for his own use or for a friend. Like the rich basketmaker, he holds himself more or less aloof from his workers and has elaborate plans for his children's future.

The various crafts were loosely organized into one omnibus guild. Like the merchant's guild, this, in its 1948 form, was a formal product of the Nationalist Government. The basic and functional units were the sub-guilds, most of which had long local histories. The head of the omnibus guild was a prominent landlord and gentleman. He was of great use in settling disputes, but his actual power was circumscribed and nominal. As in the case of the Merchant guilds, each trade fixed prizes and standardized quality; unlike the merchant sub-guilds, some of the handicraft sub-guilds were not averse to a good deal of competition. The workers in the various trades were considered represented in the guilds. Actually the workers were not organized in any effective way and they relied upon the guild to establish a fair wage for them. The wage might, indeed, vary from place to place. It depended most of all on the individual relationship between the worker and his master, in other words, on the *kanch'ing* that existed between them.

Before leaving the subject of artisans it will be well to review one specific case of a worker in order to see in relief most of the generalizations previously made. Hwa is a 17 year old carpenter's apprentice.[20] Before the war his family was doing well as tenant-farmers. When the Jap-

---

[20] The example of Hwa, the carpenter's apprentice in Ch'u may be compared with Li Po-lin, the pickling-works apprentice in Chengtu. See Liao, 1948.

anese came the family fled into the countryside where its members stayed for over a year. When they returned to Ch'uhsien they found that their house had been destroyed and that their lease-land was now being cultivated by a new tenant. The boy's father then managed to get a job as a clerk in a store selling candles and incense. He saved enough to send his son to school for a few years but finally could not stand the expense of further education. The father would like to see the boy return to school after his apprenticeship but this is just a pious hope. The boy became an apprentice after his father convinced a carpenter friend that the boy would be a good worker. He now lives with the carpenter and is given three good meals a day. Once a year he gets a suit of clothes from his *laopan* but he is fortunate in getting other clothes and sundries from his father. His laundry is done by his mother, thus avoiding an expense which plagues the budgets of most apprentices. He is very fortunate in that he has proved a good worker and the *kan-ch'ing* between his employer and his father has become better. When business is good he gets the equivalent of US 2c or 3c a day which he can save or spend as he chooses. Since regular carpenter's wages are relatively high he would like to continue in carpentry but he is not certain that he will get the opportunity. Hwa's apprenticeship is not quite typical, since he works within easy distance of his parents' home. The services and benefits which he gets directly from home are not normally available to the apprentice. Even in the case of Hwa, however, he spends his period of apprenticeship largely in a world of non-kin related persons. His adjustments are made to strangers and take place within a framework of social forms based on specific levels and techniques of production, they do not take their form after any set of kin patterns.

TENANTS AND CONSUMERS

Our previous categories have been consistent in taking their character from distinct and comparable functions in the system of production in Ch'uhsien. Likewise, the groups to follow, which include the gentry and the bureaucracy, also may be described by their techniques of gaining subsistence and by such surpluses they may succeed in amassing. The present category, however, is based on a somewhat different set of criteria revolving about consumption and actually may include members of all the other groups discussed. As a matter of fact, the prime topic of this section is a tenant's council which was formed to protest the rising rentals of Ch'u houses, and that council included members of almost all the groups we have already discussed as well as certain petty officials.

In June, 1948, after extensive rumor, a proclamation began to appear all over Ch'u. This announcement was printed on a large piece of paper and was nailed or pasted to doors and walls in every street. The following is a translation of the text:

NOTICE OF ESTABLISHMENT
TENANT ASSOCIATION
CH'U HSIEN

This association was formally established on June 3, 1948 after the approval of the Ch'u Hsien Government. We are afraid that the name of this new organization will arouse misunderstanding in part of the people. Therefore we want to explain to the public the purpose and function of this association. Since V-J Day the housing situation in this hsien has been very serious. Furthermore, due to the high density of population, the supply of houses has never been able to meet the demand. As a result, a sharp increase in house rent took place, and the rent has even been changed [from money] to rice. The monthly rent per room has ranged from two or three *tou*[21] of rice to six to seven *tou*. There are exceptions but the exceptions are very few where the rent was maintained at the pre-war level of one *tou* of rice per room as in the houses of Mr. Han Ming-chu on Lou Tung Street and the houses of Mr. Hsu Yueh-ya and Mr. Chin Yen-shen on South Street. During the time when the price of rice is soaring high, the members of this association feel that they cannot afford to shoulder the burden, especially in the cases of poor government employees and refugees. If [these conditions] are going to prevail, the lives of the majority of the people will be menaced and social disturbance may possibly arise. The organizers of this association, in view of the seriousness of the above problem, have proposed since last year to form a tenant association with the following purposes: (1) to arbitrate the disputes between landlords and tenants with reasonable measures. (2) To seek for the general welfare of the members by reasonable steps. Fortunately we have achieved success in this respect. Henceforth we will adhere to the above principles and render our service to all concerned parties, landlords and their tenants in the hsien with a view to reasonably solving the problems of rental.

In the joint meeting of the boards of directors and supervisors, the following resolution was passed: The payment of rent of the members of the association will be made with 40% discount according to the former rice rent price paid in cash. This has aroused surprise in some quarters which have thought that this association deprived the landlord of his [profit]. Much criticism has been made by the local populace. They do not know that to base the house rent directly on rice is against the law. Before the joint conference passed this

---

[21] One *tou* in Ch'u Hsien equals 13 and 1/3 pounds. (The *tou* is normally a volume measure, here adapted for clarity.)

resolution we received a dispatch from the Ch'u Hsien Hsien Government (#4172 to the People's Society) saying that the calculation of rent in all the places in China should be made according to the method of calculation in Nanking according to a circular instruction from the Executive Yuan. At that time the members of the board of directors and supervisors, although they understood that this was a legal standard, still thought that the establishment of landlords' and tenants' *kan-ch'ing* arising from economic cooperation and the spirit of human friendliness [was of greatest importance].

The land census of the hsien was started over two years ago. Ten percent of the annual profits, based on the price structure at the time of land registration, was to be paid as rent. But today such payment would be insufficient. . . . Therefore we have adopted the resolution [to discount 40%] which was actually a concession to the landlord. We did not neglect the feelings of either side and we adapted the law to human reason. We considered the landlords and tenants as one body and the resolution ruled, furthermore, that the amount of rice would remain as it was in order to respect the contracts already drawn up among the parties though, in fact, any contract which violates the law is not binding. The payment of 60% in cash was recommended in view of the [Executive Yuan order]. . . . If this is considered unfair, then where is justice? At the present time society is disturbed and the people are suffering from depression. The life of mankind can only be safeguarded by sacrificing the small self and contributing to the big self. Therefore the association will do its utmost with the greatest determination to enforce the above decision. The personal disputes which might require the meditation of this association will also be handled with fairness and justice.

Finally: I, the head of the association, returned to Ch'u Hsien [after V-J Day] and participated in educational work. I seldom attended local public affairs. This time I was elected by the members of the association as the director-general and found it impossible to refuse. I will do my utmost to follow the members of the association in rendering social service, hoping that in the shortest period of time our work may, to some extent, be fulfilled. At that time I will resign and let some better person succeed to my post. I hope that all the people in this place will give their advice on these problems so we may fulfill our mission.

Good health.

Respectfully,

Li Hsiang-yu (seal)

The proclamation of Mr. Li Hsiang-yu caused a great excitement in the population of Ch'u. Arguments, pro and con, were to be heard on all sides. Mostly, however, the town waited to see what the outcome would be. They had not long to wait. The magistrate quickly advised the Tenant Association to disband and to conduct their business as individuals. In this the landlords concurred, and since I was located in one of the richest stores in the city I heard many landlords state that they would be very receptive to individual petitions but that they abhorred group coercion. The Tenant Association, however, stood fast, and posted more of their announcements. They were not totally without influential support. Mr. Li, their director, was a respected middle-school teacher, and the three landlords mentioned in the text of their announcement as exemplary were all prominent, one of them especially so, since he was the father of Han Li-wu then Vice-minister of Education in Nanking and delegate to the National Assembly which elected Li Tsung-jen vice-president. The first pressure was put upon some of the prominent sympathizers. They were threatened with the loss of political backing. With the innuendo that they were sympathetic to the Communists steadily rising, the backers beat a quick retreat. The magistrate then moved from 'advice' to direct order and the association was commanded to disband. It did so, covering its own retreat and face with the statement that the landlords had promised to honor, on a *kan-ch'ing* basis, individual requests for rent relief. The entire movement was dead within a month.

The panorama of rent protest, social action, and the attack on this action took place in a setting of non-kin oriented relationships. The model for the tenant organization was clearly derived not from any extension or expansion of kinship alignments but obviously looked to the structure of the guilds for its guide. The reaction among the landlords took shape, not as a union of blood relatives but along class and non-kin lines. The tactics were political and all of the contacts took place in a framework of non-kin relationships. That the attempt failed does not discredit the thesis. The mere fact that such an extensive series of actions could be taken, linking together strangers in what for many was a direct attack on some pre-existing tie of kinship, is proof of the extent, in Ch'u, of non-kin ties as the effective basis of social action.

Cooperative movements of either producers or consumers in Ch'uhsien are rare but not totally absent. For the most part, Ch'uhsien moves along in a two-level economy. The bulk of the production is accomplished by individuals who control separate and discrete plants. The labor utilized is, in part, the normal number of persons supplied by the family, or in some cases, by the extended kinship units which act as a reservoir. Even more important as a source of labor, however, are the non-related individuals who are hired or brought into the productive apparatus by ties of friendship, having themselves no tie of kinship with the owner or manager of the enterprise. A slim minority is occupied at work even though their original contact with the enterprise was not preceeded by either kin or friendship ties, their first approach having been made as strangers. The second level of the economy, which we have mentioned, is that of the large number of individuals who performed no productive labor functions and yet who reaped a goodly portion of the labor return. Thus in the agrarian situation we have the landlord who supplies only the soil and the usurer who advances capital, both dealing in most instances with persons unrelated to themselves. In the city, the *laopan* of a prosperous handicraft industry is in a similar position. Hiring many persons who have no tie of kinship with him, he presents them witth work and receives the greater share of their return. The combined form of enterprise, which would see a number of individuals bound together on an equal basis and sharing all the functions of a business, including the production and distribution of the product and the sharing of the return, is not present in Ch'u.

Cooperatives in other parts of China have been discussed elsewhere in anthropologically oriented studies. A formally organized silk cooperative is described by Fei;[22] a type of handicraft industry which shows a few features of the cooperative without being a true cooperative is described by Fei and Chang.[23] Yits'un, the site of the latter example, however, is a one clan town[24] and Fei's statement "Industry in the villages of the interior is bound by family organi-

---

[22] Fei, 1938, pp. 216-225.   [23] Fei and Chang, 1945, pp. 178-181.
[24] Ibid., p. 133.

zation. It cannot be planned or managed in the most rational way,"[25] should be understood in this context. At that, the statement must be amended to fit even the local situation, as Fei hastens to add, "Since the owner cannot operate his mill the whole year, he rents it, either through friendship or for profit, to others who possess raw materials."[26] The factors which directly limit folk-industrial development are the availability of raw materials and labor; familism, according to Fei's own evidence, is secondary and its effects are avoidable. The closest approach to a marketing cooperative in Ch'u is the partnership which we have described in some details above.

Two further movements in the direction of cooperatives should be mentioned. First, in order to increase the productivity of the *hsien,* to extend the effective area of land utilization and to promote a campaign designed to curtail banditry, a plan was devised by the local govenment with the assistance of a visiting agricultural expert of the Christian Church as well as with the aid of the local missionary, calling for the resettlement of tenants. Rent and taxes were suspended on this land and the farmers were to be organized into a cooperative self-defense unit.[27] Cooperation in the utilization of local labor along lines described in the previous chapter, was also to be encouraged. At first the cooperation was to be on a relatively formal basis to compensate for the newness of the relationships among the neighbors. There was also pressure on the part of the Christian advisors for a marketing cooperative, but the local gentry did nothing to further these plans.

---

[25] Ibid., p. 193.   [26] Ibid., p. 193.
[27] Compare the cooperative self-defense unit described by Yang, 1945, p. 180.

At the behest of the Central Goverment, which had sent a specialist in cooperative organization into Ch'u in 1947, a small consumer cooperative was set up near the center of Ch'u. This small store was designed to furnish the officials of Ch'u with foodstuffs and certain other basic essentials. The plan called for the supply of these items at cost plus a bare profit to enable the shop to expand. It was to be supplied by Nanking and supplemented by favor from the merchant guild. The shop was never a success. It was always poorly stocked and its goods were said to be inferior. When business continued poorly its prices were raised in an effort to recoup the losses sustained. The enterprise was still functioning when I left Ch'u but did a minimum of sales. It was no longer even a curiosity for the populace.[28]

---

[28] Many studies have been made by Chinese social scientists of modern cooperatives in China. See, Yang, H. K., 1927; Djang, Y. S., 1931; Cheng Lin-chuang, 1937; etc.

non-kin forces among the gentry

The Chinese gentry may be distinguished by a number of related criteria among which are leisure, non-productive occupation,[1] literacy, and high status.[2] The gentry has often been thought of as most dependent of all Chinese

---

[1] For those who object to "non-productive occupation" as a criterion of gentry identification and who contend with Max Weber and others that managerial functions are productive, certain amplification is in order. While managerial functions may supplement technological forces of production thereby increasing output or channelling it more effectively, they tend to do so only at certain points in the social process. This progressive role of managerial status occurs primarily during periods of transition from one major system to another. Thereafter managerial roles tend to degenerate in that their main function becomes the protection of a traditional network of privileges and prerogatives. The latter was the case with the Chinese gentry at the time of my study, as it had been for ages in the past. As landlords the gentry guarded their rents, as officials they extended their tax demands and further guarded their rents. In none of this did they act to increase production, rather a case may be made for the role of the gentry in lowering production and opposing efforts to expand it.

[2] Fei, 1946, p. 10: Fei and Chang, 1945, pp. 246-47: Lang, 1945, p. 6.

groupings on relationships which stem from the extension of the kin principle. Thus Fei Hsiao-tung has stated:

I think that both the big-family (or the house) system and the clan are the gentry's organizations . . . and the most elaborate and effective clans are found in the gentry . . . In China it is the gentry who find it necessary, in order to be powerfully organized, to employ the principle of kinship extensively.[3]

Others have stated similar opinions. Olga Lang has described extensive kin relationships among the gentry as accoutrements of wealth rather than as techniques of continuing aggrandizement.[4] My own view in this matter is closer to the one held by Lang than that expressed in the citations from Fei. Fei's statement may result, in part, from his oversight of some of the most evident details of Chinese society. It has often been said that one of the advantages of the anthropologist's technique is that it sets to work in one culture a man of another culture. The observer, finding all to be new, does not suffer the blindness of familiarity. This may partially explain how Fei can overlook the great extent of non-kin relationships in commerce, religion, education, production, and other phases of Chinese life.

One of my gentry friends in Ch'u was fond of the well known Chinese proverb, "Distant relatives are not as valuable as near-by friends." He grew especially fond of the proverb when the conflicting desires of his relatives almost drove him to ruin. The gentleman in question was Mr. Chang, who found himself unable to bury his grand-

---

[3] Fei, 1946, p. 5-6.   [4] Lang, 1945, p. 180.

mother without plunging into debt. Due to the heavy taxation he had already been obliged to mortgage several fields which he had small hope of recovering, and further to mortgage land would have resulted in disaster. He had a position as secretary in the local Christian mission, though he himself was not a Christian, and his income from this position, over long enough time, would enable him to reach some sort of budgetary stasis. When his grandmother died, he was anxious to bury her with a minimum of pomp but his mother and a host of paternal relatives objected. The house became a hotbed of argument and complaint, so much so that Mr. Chang spent more and more time away from home, with the writer and with a group of friends. Each night, though, he returned to his home, since any other course was unthinkable, and each night the pressures were repeated. Finally, the conflict having raged for several months before the old lady's death, he gave in only a few hours after the grandmother's demise. When he went to buy a suitable coffin, scrolls, paper effigies, music and other funeral necessities, he discovered, of course, that his money was insufficient. After selling the small rice surplus which he had carefully saved from the rents which had been collected, he discovered himself still to be short. Mr. Chang now started to canvass his relatives for funds. Most relatives pleaded poverty or in other ways avoided giving money. One, a rice speculator, gave a token loan at no interest but said that a further loan would be made at usual usurious terms. Mr. Chang could not afford to take this loan. Some help was forthcoming at the Ch'u Hsien County Bank where a second cousin was the director. He granted a small loan at terms, which, in view of the inflation, were interest free.

After all of the relatives had been approached, Mr. Chang was still behind his quota. At this point, he turned to his friends. Most of them were young men like himself, small landlords, teachers and petty officials. None of them refused him. Some gave only token amounts but among the rest he was enabled to borrow, without interest, enough money to see him through the emergency. When the funeral was held, most of the relatives were found to have given gifts of spirit money, the cheapest funeral offering which can be made. Mr. Chang was quite bitter but said that it merely bore out the old proverb, the truth of which he had always known.

The instance of Mr. Chang may be extreme, and, in the last analysis, it is important that he exhausted the resources of his relatives (as far as they were cooperative) before turning to non-kin contacts. But he did resort to friends and those friends made an excellent display of solidarity. Let us turn for the moment to those friends, identify them, show how the friendships came about, how they operated, and how they fit into the larger social patterns.

Though it is true that, as Lang says, a wealthy man attracts relatives so that he may number the persons related to him who come for aid in the hundreds,[5] it is also true that the urban gentleman is far ahead of the peasant or the worker in his opportunity for fruitful non-kin contacts. As a child, the young city dweller operates in a large group of play-mates particularly if he is male. The average child plays in a group which includes some related individuals, but, in most cases, also plays with non-related

---

5 Lang, 1945, p. 167.

children. Though these play contacts last for several years, few permanent alignments take shape. The first major area within which a large number of permanent non-kin contacts are set up is in the school group. Within Ch'uhsien in 1947-48 there were two kinds of elementary schools. One was the new 'public' school which had many branches and charged variable tuition rates while teaching a curriculum geared to the changing Chinese scene. The other type of school was traditional, consisting of a one room schoolhouse and one teacher. The traditional curriculum was little altered, consisting in largest part of learning the classics by rote. (One teacher in a small rural school excitedly told me that his school was modern and taught only the latest things. When I watched his class I found them reciting verbatim texts from geography and history books. The subject matter had changed somewhat but the techniques were ancient.) The new type of schools have a class arrangement whereby the students at each year level are taught separately. Association in age-class groups facilitates the formation of friendships which furnish the nuclei of cliques. The two factors which operate in the formation of these friendships are identity of class and proximity of residence. The cliques are of two kinds. One type operates completely within the neighborhood and consists of boys who are cementing previous friendships through common experiences in school. The other has its life within the school and brings together boys who live in relatively distant neighborhoods. The importance of these friendships becomes greater as the child grows older. When he graduates, he often finds himself tied to a few or many of his classmates by strong emotional and common interest bonds. Many of these friendships will weaken and become moribund but hardly any will die completely. After many years the mention of common participation in a class in elementary school will serve to erect a bridge between strangers. Many boys go on with the friendships made in school until they even challenge the kinship structure for loyalty.

The most important level of education within which friendships are created is the middle school. Ch'u has two middle schools, junior and senior, and in both there is a certain feeling for school-class membership that surpasses the mere period of attendance and sets up a long range contact. Thus, while in Ch'u I was invited several times to class reunions or class outings. Much time was spent accompanying informants to the houses of their friends and in many instances these friends traced their acquaintanceship to middle-school. In the affairs of Mr. Chang, as related above, the friends he approached for financial aid were all of the same middle school graduating class. These friends not only maintain contact with each other when they continue to reside in the same city or area but also maintain correspondence when separated by distance. In some instances, old school friends are used as valuable stepping stones to positions in a new place and even in Ch'u the importance of these school friends in aiding one to get a new position cannot be overrated.

When a man goes on to college, he continues to make friends but, at least for the man who comes from a small interior city, these friendships are often not as important as those which he made in school. Many a man of Ch'u who is a college graduate has returned from the university to pick up the thread of his life in Ch'u. In such cases the man gravitates toward those others about him who have also been college educated. Most of these people will, of course, be the wealthier of his former middle school chums and acquaintances, and older contacts will be reinforced. Though the large cities like Shanghai and Peiping have formal clubs for the graduates of the various universities, as well as specialized clubs for overseas students, the college students have no formal organization in Ch'u. None of the school associations are formal; they have no by-laws or officials. Their interaction is based on the mutual attraction of interested persons and the institutionalized expression of group unity is the outing, generally to Lang-ya Mountain for a picnic lunch at the Buddhist monastery.

LANDLORD DEPENDENCE ON OUTSIDE: ECONOMIC

The landlord gentry are enmeshed in many non-kin relationships which are far more pervasive than those described above. The most elementary connection between the landlord and his subsistence involves a host of individuals who are not related to him by blood. They are joined, instead, by ties of mutual interest. I have already given many of these ties in some detail but the stress has been placed upon the position of the farmer in these complexes. To show the nature of the ties as seen by the landlord we may repeat some factors, each time in a new light.

On my return from China I had occasion to discuss some of my field materials with an ethnologist whose specialty was an area geographically removed from the scene of my investigations. During the discussion of the subsistence of the population of Ch'u, when the method of securing the basic foodstuffs was detailed, the ethnologist became somewhat confused. Her questions revolved about a single point; were not the landlords and the tenants ultimately related and was not the passage of food from farm to city house part of a system of reciprocal social behavior based on this kinship? The fact is that very few of the landlords in Ch'uhsien are even distantly related to their tenants. In those cases in which a blood relationship exists, such landlord-tenant relationships differ in slight detail, if at all, from the non-related norm.[6] In these cases kinship can be as much of a hindrance as a help. The existence of bonds which are felt as binding by the landlord cannot be denied, and the landlord is morally in such a position that he must aid his poorer relatives by renting them land. Once on the land, the kin relationship should restrain the landlord in the matter of rent collection. Such is the ideal. In reality, the landlord would avoid letting land to any relative he thought might grow burdensome. If he did rent out the land to such a relative he would give him no more special consideration than he would give any tenant who was unrelated by blood but who had cultivated excellent *kan-ch'ing*.

The landlord lives largely on the rents he collects from his lands. The tenant who cultivates this earth and who pays the landlord forty percent of his crop is generally not related to the landlord. The landlord's prime dependence in the matter of subsistence falls clearly on his relationship with a non-relative. We shall turn, in just a moment, to a view of the sanctions which maintain this structure; before that, however, it is well to point out that any

---

[6] Similar observations are made in Fei and Chang, 1945, p. 226.

income beyond that supplied by rents also depends to a great extent on non-kin relationships. The landlord cultivates nothing; if he has any way of increasing his income, it is through employment in government service or through commerce. His dependence on the outside as an official is described below; his dependence as a member of the commercial world on a system of relationships extending into the outside has been illustrated above. In any direction that he may turn, he faces a world of discrete and non-related entities like himself. In some instances he attempts to bridge the gaps among these entities by extending, as far as possible, the simple and pre-existing ties of kinship. In most instances, however, these ties are found to be functionally insufficient and the major burden of effective connection is carried by a large system of non-kin ties.

This system of non-kin relationships is clearly reflected in microcosm in the dependence of the landlord-gentleman on the outside for the satisfaction of needs which he considers basic to his subsistence. To illuminate this matter I will present some material drawn from sample budgets collected from Ch'u landlords.

Every day, Mr. B. uses certain commodities for himself and his family. From his tenants he gets rice. In the markets and shops of Ch'u he spends cash and receives vegetable oil and lard for ordinary cooking, fuel-grass, matches, kerosene, water, and fresh vegetables. During the course of a normal month he will also buy pork, beef, poultry, eggs, salt, fish, and tea from stores and markets. Some of these things, such as eggs and poultry may come to him as a present from a tenant but this is rare, occurring institutionally only in conjunction with certain holidays. Also, among the things which will be consumed during the course of a year are clothing, lamp glasses, ceremonial paraphernalia and gifts. Of these items only a few may be made at home. Mr. B's wife makes cloth shoes out of remnants and she may make some items of clothing. However, today almost all the cloth is bought in stores and, actually, very few women of this class make men's clothing, a professional tailor being hired instead. Finally, there is a large category of expenses which are regular and institutional in nature. Among them are house rents in the city, taxes, ceremonial expenses, servant's wages or support, and possible payments for the education of one or more members of the family. Clearly the landlord-gentleman is not only insufficient within his family and extended kin unit but is actually totally dependent on an advanced and well integrated economy, operating in which, he finds most of his contacts with outsiders.

In many of these contacts the parties concerned operate on a face-to-face but completely impersonal level. Thus, the landlord in marketing does not set up any regular association with a specific seller of cabbage or water chestnuts; as a matter of fact, such marketing is frequently delegated to a servant or is done by a woman of the household. When the servant is the one who does the shopping a relatively stable relationship does often develop between buyer and seller. I refer to the system of rebating on the purchase, whereby the servant and the clerk make an informal compact by which they divide part of the price of an item. This system, many foreigners will be astounded to know, has plagued Chinese employers as well as Europeans, though it is more typical in a large Chinese city than in such a small interior setting.

Under the old, pre-inflation, credit system of buying there was a frequent development of something approaching friendship between a merchant and a steady customer. This relationship was of advantage to both parties in its encouragement of the growth of *kan-ch'ing*. It made possible a number of deepening contacts which superceded the simple ties of trade and which now might become permanent, thus extending the mutual exchange of help in the placement and security of related individuals or friends and the exchange of credit or other facilities.[7] During the period of inflation, when supplies were reduced and a black market arose in consumer's goods, well established relationships of this type became a prime medium, in the general absence of effective bonds of kin, of protection from the adverse effects of a collapsing economy.

----

7 Compare Durkheim who was primarily interested in the most dramatic and completely institutionalized forms of interpersonal relationships and frequently missed important social phenomena of a lower order of integration: ". . . individuals working at the same trade have relations with one another because of their similar occupation. Even competition puts them in relationship. But these relations have nothing ordered about them; they depend upon chance meetings, and have, very often, an entirely personal aspect. A particular tradesman is found in contact with some fellow-tradesman; this does not result from the industrial body of this or that specialty united for common action. In exceptional circumstances, the members of the same occupation come together as a unit to treat some question of general interest, but these meetings are only temporary. They do not survive the particular circumstances which bring them into being, and consequently the collective life of which they are the cause is more or less completely obliterated with them." Durkheim, 1933, p. 6.

LANDLORD DEPENDENCE ON OUTSIDE: POLITICAL

Though the landlords must purchase many of the staple items on which they subsist from a formally organized market, their ultimate dependence is on the recognition by the tenants of the obligation of paying rent. Some landlords manage to supplement their incomes from sources other than the collection of tenants' dues. For example, one of the richest gentlemen in Ch'u made his fortune in speculations outside of Ch'uhsien. However, for most landlords the basic resource which supplies both food and the money to trade for other commodities and services is the labor of the tenant farmers.

The typical rent in Ch'uhsien, as we have seen, is 40% of the staple crops. When this payment has been made and when the farmer attends to such other indebtedness as he may have incurred, as well as the operating and ceremonial expenses which normally are involved in farm management, he is frequently in a position of obvious insecurity, the potential victim of the first emergency which may arise. Why under such conditions, it may be asked, does the tenant continue payments which threaten his very existence?

Three factors operate in this question; continuity, polity and coercion. The first is informal and involves the "cake of custom." The consideration is phrased as a moral one, sanctified by time and usage and exemplified by the remarks of some tenants of Kaihsienkung in Kiangsu Province:

"We are good people. We never refuse to pay our rent. We cannot steal even when we are poor. How then can we refuse to pay rent?"

"... Why do you pay rent?" ... "The landlord owns the land. We cultivate his land. We only have the land surface. The surface cannot exist without the subsoil."[8]

Ch'uhsien lacks the concept of top- and sub-soil rights but conversations similar in all other respects might have been recorded there. Such attitudes, as Fei points out, are largely, but not totally, confined to the old people. The younger folk show more regard for power and sanctions than for demands which are merely customary. The simple desire for maintainance of old ways does not operate alone. It is constantly reinforced by ties which might be called reciprocal. But this reciprocity does not imply either symmetrical or mutually equivalent behavior on the part of the participants[9] as is the case, for example, in the Trobriands, where,

Most if not all economic acts are found to belong to some chain of reciprocal gifts and counter-gifts, which in the long run balance, *benefiting both sides equally.* ...

The real reason why all these economic obligations are normally kept, and kept very scrupulously, is that the failure to comply places a man in an intolerable position, while slackness in fulfillment covers him with opprobrium.[10]

Nor yet, on this level of analysis, may this phenomenon be described as "unilateral,"[11] since there are certain semi-institutionalized aspects of mutual exchange involving

---

8 Fei, 1939, p. 189.
9 Just as egalitarian kinship characterizes societies on certain simple levels of productivity and does not operate in modern complex societies, so true reciprocity as conceived by Malinowski does not seem to apply to modern societies but only to simple and kin-based ones.
10 Malinowski, 1926, p. 40-41 (my emphasis.) 11 Cf Durkheim, 1933, p. 180.

such customs as the granting of a small section of land to the tenant upon which he may grow vegetables or tobacco without paying additional rent. The landlord also, in many cases, helps with the construction or repair of a tenant's house and though this service may be mentioned in the original agreement, the actual services extend beyond this compact in accordance with the *kan-ch'ing* between the parties. The dues of the tenant, above and beyond the normal payment of rent, have already been mentioned; they include gifts and services, particularly at holiday times.

The foregoing is not concerned with the polity of the landlord-tenant relationship except as each element mentioned is sanctified by contract and upheld by authority. In the two remaining patterns, which sanction the flow of rent to the landlord, a more overt political orientation is seen. Thus, for one thing, both peasants and tenant farmers *must* cultivate the good will of the gentry because

. . . it is clear that, as long as the peasants live in the (traditional) structure, they have to rely on the gentry for protection against the encroachment of the absolute ruler and his officials.[12]

The assiduous cultivation of *kan-ch'ing* with the landlord by the tenant is evident in data which have been previously examined. One of the basic conditions which produce this relationship has been stated by an anonymous Chinese social scientist:

In spite of the landlord's right to evict his tenant uncondi-

---

[12] Fei, 1946, p. 9.

tionally [in Kwanyun, Kiangsu], the tenant usually feels quite secure on account of his personal relations with the landlord.[13]

The non-renting peasantry has less obvious ties to the gentry. One Chinese economist, however, has set the stage for the relationships between the peasants and the gentry in this fashion:

Each farming household (over a large part of China) uses the land as it sees fit, except in so far as it is influenced by the requirements of landlords, tax authorities, creditors, and, of course, the state of the market. In some parts of the country, one or other of these indirect controls is at times as effective as would be a government order enforced by police power. There are even occasions when such power practically is applied, as was the case so extensively when the tax on opium was a large item in the National and the provincial government's revenue.[14]

In Ch'uhsien it was the fashion for landlords, visiting their tenants in the countryside, to be invited for tea, wine, or a meal by neighbors of the tenants. These people hoped in this way to widen their circle of influential contacts. Many farmers, when pressed by local tax collectors or representatives of the army, would come to Ch'u where they tried to get their landlords or such influential people as they knew to intercede for them. In the Ch'uhsien of 1947-48, however, most landlords were almost as powerless as their tenants.

Warm relations with the landlords and creditors were necessary in order to gain protection from the deprada-

---

13 Chinese Economic Journal, 1927, p. 372.

14 Fong, 1937, p. 931.

tions of the outside, and many techniques were developed to cement such relationships. Of course, one of the first things that has to be done when cultivating a landlord or creditor, whether in Ch'uhsien or in Brooklyn, is to make sure that, where possible, all reasonable demands for payment are met.

There is a third element which sanctions the proper payment of rents and obligations. It is in this third factor that one can see most clearly the degree to which not only the peasant and the tenant, but also the gentleman, is bound to a system which far exceeds the microcosmic and atomistic world of family structures and kin extensions. In Ch'uhsien as in Kaihsienkung, in Anhwei as in Yunnan and Kwangtung and most areas of China, the final and ultimate sanction behind the continued and regular payment of rents and other obligations is force; the force of a state structure. The point has been variously stated by those who have done work in this field. In Kiangsu, Fei Hsiao-tung discovered that "if the tenant refuses to pay, the agent has power to arrest him and put him into the prison of the district government."[15] Fei noted the increase of conflict between landlords and tenants, "The district jail has been repeatedly crowded with default cases. Organized action of the peasants in refusing rent payments has provoked serious conflict with the landlords who are backed by government force."[16] Other observers are not so objective in their wording:

Suppose the tenant is in arrears: our landlord has all the forces of law and order behind him if he decides that it is best to evict the tenant and to take back the land with all the

---

[15] Fei, 1939, p. 189.   [16] *Ibid.*, p. 191.

improvements the tenant may have made. Or, on the other hand, he also has the authorities on his side if he decides to tide over the tenant by forcing him into a loan agreement or into the signing of a new lease which puts him completely into the hands of his creditor, the landlord himself . . . (The landlord) has at his disposal the police and military power of the district and, if need be, of the whole province; or he can hire a gang of his own to beat the workers into submission without anyone being able to stay his hands.[17]

The author of that passage, Chen Han-seng, was referring to the agrarian situation in southeast China where land hunger was greatest and where the abuses of the landlords caused the great peasant revolts of the twenties. But in Fei's town of Kaihsienkung in Kiangsu, there was a peasant revolt in 1935[18] and in Ch'uhsien, though there was no actual shooting war between landlords and tenants, there were many peripheral areas in the county which, away from the police power of the county seat, defied the landlords and paid no rent. In such instances the rents were frequently collected by an armed squad of the local militia, or even, on special occasion, by a unit of the Nationalist Army, which accompanied the agent or landlord.

Here is the crux of the matter. The landlord does not find himself surrounded by a hierarchy of political officials who are related to him by blood. It is a very lucky man indeed who can point to a single well placed official and claim a degree of kinship close enough to warrant aid. The more usual form of political relationship, in the case of the landlords, is built on a network of friendships and *kan-ch'ing*, butressed, where possible, with claims of kin-

----

17 Chen Han-seng, 1936, p. 65.   18 Fei, 1939, p. 191.

ship and cemented with economic favors. Investigations in other parts of China support this contention. In the work of Chen Han-seng we read of the

... *Tso-ke* system which necessitates an extra rent payment. A *Tso-ke* is simply a descendant of a rich merchant or a powerful official who was able to protect the small landowner against heavy taxation by having the power to defy government authorities. As a price for the protection, the small land-owner used to offer him a certain amount of grain every year, which in the course of time has come to be considered as a regular rent.[19]

On the other hand, in Yunnan, where Fei and Chang found that the tenants received special concessions if they were related to the landlord, and even in the case of the relationship of a landlord and a non-related tenant "the scales are weighted somewhat in the favor of the tenant,"[20] the conclusion validates our assumption, for in the words of Fei and Chang:

The protected position of the tenant in Luts'un is in strik-ing contrast to the situation in coastal China, where he is almost entirely at the mercy of the landlord. The reasons are found in the small number of individual landlords, who are, moreover, small owners and hence not powerful, and in (other) factors ... which serve as checks on the power of the group owners.[21]

It can be clearly seen that the power of the landlord to control the collection of rents rests on a series of relation-ships that only occasionally correlate with the kinship

19 Chen Han-seng, 1936, pp. 59-60.
20 Fei and Chang, 1945, p. 79.
21 Fei and Chang, op. cit., p. 80.

system. In this non-familial political system, an individual may improve his position by manipulating kin ties, but the system itself is quite independent of elementary kin orientation; thus the careful cultivation of the good will and sympathy of an official is an important part of the life of a typical gentleman. We have already seen, in an earlier chapter, how kinship with an official or army officer can be used to alleviate the pressures of taxation. But similar results can be obtained in the absence of kinship by the cultivation of favorable *kan-ch'ing*. Thus, Mr. B., the *laopan* of a great store, assiduously courted the county magistrate, entertaining him and giving gifts and favors. Mr. B. also sought to ingratiate himself with the military by currying favor with higher officers. He took great pains to patronize even the humble soldiers and over-subscribed many of the military requisitions. In return, he was spared many indignities of quartering, being asked to house only officers, and the military police helped keep order in the store whenever a scarce commodity was put on limited scale.

Mr. Chang had no influential relatives close enough to be valuable. One cousin was a petty bureaucrat in the *hsien* government but of little help. However, the secretary to the magistrate was a middle-school classmate of Mr. Chang and he was called upon to a limited degree. As a matter of fact, the secretary was disliked by most of his classmates because he had entered government service direct from middle school and had never gone to college. Despite this fact, he had, in 1947 and 1948, one of the most influential positions of his entire middle school graduating class. His attitude was one of superiority and grudging friendship. He accepted all of his friends' invitations but never reciprocated. After he left a meeting or a banquet and he always was the first to leave, the man who remained would talk about him in the most unflattering terms. However, he was fairly important to all of them, since, being the protégé of the magistrate, he had that official's complete confidence. The secretary was used several times by Mr. Chang and others in order to get small concessions on the payment of taxes or levies, particularly in the matter of overdue payments.

LANDLORD DEPENDENCE ON OUTSIDE: RELIGIOUS AND OTHER

Unlike the farmer, the landlord does not have a temple to the earth god as a center of his worship. Instead, his fortunes are believed to revolve about the maintenance of a family shrine. The major religious devotions of a Ch'uhsien gentleman are largely confined to this family shrine and it may be said that, of all the areas discussed, religion continues to be that of greatest self-sufficiency. Yet, even here, there are gaps which are filled not by kin dependent ties but by the links of a more complex social structure. The previous analysis of birth ceremonials, weddings and funerals explicitly demonstrated the importance of kin ties in delineating the ceremonial group as well as the importance of the ties of friendship and neighborhood. The ties between friends and neighbors have been held important in Chinese society from the days of old and the virtues of friendliness have been celebrated in the Ores, in the Analects of Confucius and elsewhere:

From the Son of Heaven down to the multitudes of the people, there is no one but needs friends in order to his own perfection. When a ruler by his affection for his kindred makes them harmonious, when he makes friends of men of worth and does not foresake them, when he does not forget his old associates, then the people become truly virtuous[22]

Tsze Kung pursued, 'I venture to ask who may be placed in the next lower rank of officers?' and he was told, 'He whom the circle of his relatives pronounce to be filial, whom his fellow villagers and friends pronounce to be fraternal.'[23]

The master said 'Virtue is not left to stand alone. He who practices it will have neighbors.'[24]

There is even one ode which offers a mild rebuke to those who have been neglecting the ties of kin in favor of the bonds of friendship:

> . . . of all the men in the world
> There are none equal to brothers.
>
> Brothers may quarrel inside the walls,
> But they will oppose insult from without,
> When friends, however good they may be,
> Will not afford help.
>
> When death and disorder are past,
> And there are tranquility and rest;
> Although they have brothers,
> (Some) reckon them not equal to friends.[25]

Though the most important ceremonials are confined to the home, the equipment used in house worship, including incense, candles, candelebra, and some of the stuff of sacrifice is bought from the outside. The guide for the

---

[22] Legge, 1871, vol. XV., pt. I, p. 63 (Little Preface).
[23] Legge, 1861, Book XIII, Ch. 20:2, p. 135.
[24] Legge, 1861, vol. I., Book IV, Ch. 25, p. 36.
[25] Legge, 1871, vol. IV., pt. II, Book I, Ode IV, pp. 250-252.

regulation of the religious year, the almanac, is bought from a vendor at the beginning of the new year. In addition, as in the cases of the farmers discussed before, there are certain occasions which see a shift of focus from the home shrine to some outside temple. The Ch'uhsien family in need of supernatural aid cannot often rely on family ties to produce it. Not one single son of a gentry family known to me in Ch'uhsien had entered the priesthoods of either the Buddhist or Taoist ranks. If one wanted the aid of the priests he went to the temple and there solicited it individually. As a matter of fact, the pressures were somewhat reversed. The beautiful old temples and monastery buildings of Lang-ya Shan had deteriorated and some had suffered from Japanese occupancy during the war. The abbot of Lang-ya wished to restore the site to its former glory and was busily soliciting funds from the merchants and gentry of Ch'u for this purpose.

The younger gentry had little or no use for the Taoist temple and its few priests, particularly the old man who headed the temple. Among women and the poorly educated he passed leaving terror behind, since he was reputed to be skilled in all kinds of magic. The most important day of the year, as far as the Taoist priest was concerned, was the holiday of the fifth day of the fifth month *(wu yüeh chieh)* on which day the evil spirits of disease are driven away. The children wear small protective aprons on which the five poisonous animals and insects are represented, and the Taoist priests moved about the town selling woodblock prints of the demon chaser, Chung K'uei. Hardly anyone, even the most outspoken of the young landlords, refuses to give something in return to the Taoist monk for fear of angering him, which might lead to disaster.

The use of the priesthood only peripherally in Buddhist and Taoist ceremonials makes formal church organization secondary.[25a] The most general type of religious activity is found in the home cults which are devoted to ancestral worship. This is in contrast to the ways of new Christian religions which have been present in Ch'uhsien less than 100 years. Two forms of Christianity are present, Roman Catholicism and Protestantism. Each has a church in Ch'u and both have a small body of adherents. The two Christian churches create in their followers a greater dependence on the outside. Unlike the native temples, which recognize no sabbath and which rarely have formal ceremonials of a general appeal, the churches have regular Sunday worship. What is more, much of their membership is composed of parts of families rather than whole family groups. In many households, conversions have been made among the young or among the women, while the older folk or the men remain aloof. The converts, as long as their interest remains high, more or less separate themselves from the regular religious life of their families. They may take part in the rites of ancestral worship, which may be permitted, but do not act in the ceremonies designed to appease or cajole the kitchen god, the god of wealth, and the general pantheon. The case with which this individualization of religious preference, which in our own culture would produce a tremendous amount

---

[25a] The most significant institutional use of Buddhist clergy occurs at funerals—and may continue beyond the period of inhumation. The financial drain of using the priests may drive individuals and families to ruin.

of aggression and conflict, is met in China, speaks well for the previous recognition of extra-kin ties, since in many cases all of the various members of a nuclear family have different religious persuasions but manage to continue functioning despite these differences. The crises arrive, not on the basis of comparison of attitudes, but on the simple question of the performance of certain rites. As has been shown above, the older generation generally wins compliance on the basis of a many faceted attack.

One last religious feature that must be mentioned is the religious society. Ch'uhsien has several of these, each with a discrete and often semi-secret or secret membership. Many of these religious organizations have, at one time or another, taken over political functions. One writer on Chinese secret societies, plagued by the problem of separating religious and political secret societies has written:

Dans l'étude de ces Sociétés, les associations forment un chapitre special. On les divise souvent en sectes religieuses et Sociétés politiques. On verra que cette distinction est, en pratique, presque toujours très difficile à faire.[26]

At any rate, the secret society binds together a large number of men who are unrelated and causes them to operate as if they were bound by the strongest of familial ties.[27] In so doing, it is assumed that the various members stand together in the relationship of sworn blood brothers in the tradition of the three heroes of the San Kuo. This is characteristic, for example, of the Triad society, which has played so great a role in the last several hundred

---

[26] Favre, 1933, p. 23.
[27] Stanton, 1900, p. 42-43.

years of Chinese history, particularly in the attempts to overthrow the Manchu rulers. Thirty-six oaths were taken by the novitiates of this society; several of them are of particular interest in the present context:

(Article 2.) When you have entered the Hung league, you ought to keep secret everything from your wife and family, for fear that something might leak out before strangers; even so that as a father, you don't tell it to your son, as an elder brother you don't tell it to your younger brother. Do not betray the secrets of the Hung-league![28]

A stronger version appears elsewhere:

3. After entering the Hung doors, you must be loyal to your chief, and not blab to your father, son, brother or other persons, nor tell them when Heaven's time for action comes. May the Five Patriarchs look down on and be witnesses against those who disregard this injunction.[29]

(Article 24.) After having entered the Hung-league, if your own brother or a relation of yours, or a friend, and a brother of the Hung-league quarrel, brawl, or fight together, you may give a signal (to call the other brethren together) , in order to exhort them to leave off. But if you separate them forcibly, and help them (the strangers) , it is a crime of conspiring with the police—may you then perish in a wretched country.[30]

A much stronger version appears elsewhere:

12. When the members of the great family are at variance with a *member's own brother he shall not help his own brother* to

---

[28] Schlegel, 1866, p. 135.
[29] Stanton, 1900, p. 61.
[30] Schlegel, 1866, p. 141.

defeat the members of the Hung family. If any brother disregard this obligation may he be cast into the great ocean.[31]

It is quite true that the Hung society considered itself
as a family and that the relationships subsumed within
the society were considered analogous to kin relationships
in the outside world. Nevertheless, the most superficial
analysis quickly destroys this simplistic self-view. The Society was composed of males exclusively and in such details
as the relationship of a sponsor to a novitiate the pattern
was not like that of father and son but instead was deliberately symbolic of the maternal-uncle and nephew relationship.[32] Indeed, in the precise articles cited above, the
true biological and social families of the member's origin
are placed securely in a secondary position even though
several other articles adjure the member in general terms
to respect the normal filial patterns.[33]

The writer collected no data on any secret Ch'uhsien
society related to the famous *Ko Lao Hui* or its branches.
The one society with which he gained minor rapport was
described by several members as purely religious in nature. It was called the *Li Chiao Hui* and was Buddhist,
being consecrated to Kuan Yin. The members held regular
meetings in one of several special private "temples," which
actually were the homes of the society's officials. The most
important days were observed with religious worship, including sacrifice and feasting, and clustered about the

----

[31] Ward and Stirling, 1925, I, p. 66, italics in source. See also, Schlegel,
op. cit., p. 154, Art. 20.
[32] Stanton, 1900, p. 43.
[33] *Ibid.*, pp. 61-69; Schlegel, 1886, pp. 135-43, 152-66: note esp. incest extensions; Ward and Stirling, 1927, I, pp. 64-70, p. 175, rule I.

"three birthdays" of Kuan Yin, the nineteenth of the third, sixth and ninth months. The society is characterized by abstention from smoking, drinking and swearing, and is said to have started in Kiangsu province about the time of the 1911 Revolution. The claim of the members, that their society was purely religious in nature, was denied by various other informants who accused the Society of protecting thieves and bandits and exerting a good deal of pressure in local politics. It was said that the society was responsible for the brief outbreak of threatening letters which plagued several of my informants, warning them to stop consorting with the foreigner. Since further investigation of this society might have jeopardized the more general study that I was conducting, the matter was not explored.

If religion, despite its tendency to center in the home, shows many features which carry out and beyond the realm of demonstrable kin ties, the same is even more true of the general social contacts of any given individual of the gentry class. I have already shown that, in the matters of practical economy, the landlord is quite likely to be forced into channels outside the home.

THE DEMANDS OF FRIENDSHIP OR *kan-ch'ing*

The friction engendered in the normal living arrangements among kinfolk often moves individuals to seek social outlets beyond the circle of blood or affinal relatives. Thus the clubs formed of classmates are vital to the well-being of a young man or woman just as older landlords preserve friendships that are based on shared enjoyment. Many of the gentry have favorite companions—one or two individuals of the same sex who have similar interests.

Most common is the pleasure which may be shared in quietly walking and conversing, or the enjoyment that is gained from contemplating the scenery from spots which are recognized for their beauty. Friendships such as these, first made in youth, might underlie a man's whole life.[34] Lang points out that "Friendship, not love, inspired the most beautiful lines in Chinese poetry,"[35] and she cites the poem *To LiChien* by Po Chu-i. Certainly friendship is stressed in the Chinese novel and even in Chinese painting.[36] The evidence leads Lang to conclude that,

> Friendship is still an essential feature of Chinese life. As of old, a good friend, "One who knows me," plays a great part in the life of a Chinese, and the man who has no close friends is as unhappy as the one who has no family—perhaps even more so.[37]

The evidence, above, has been largely concerned with the positive aspects of friendship as it might be viewed by a man of gentry status. There are also many areas in which non-kin ties operate somewhat differently. In discussing the matters which require the use of go-betweens, whether for the purpose of effecting a transfer of land or preparing the way for a marriage, non-kin ties frequently determine the selection of specific middle-men. When the owner of a large "grocery-store" and other enterprises wished to extend his holdings by building a new shop he required the services of two go-betweens to make the proper arrangements for the transfer of property. Both of

---

[34] Lin, 1949, pp. 58-59.
[35] Lang, 1945, p. 325.
[36] *Ibid.*, p. 325
[37] *Ibid.*, p. 326.

these *chung-jen* were mutual friends of both Mr. B., the buyer and Mr. C., the seller. One of the friends was an official of the local office of the Bank of China, the other was a local scholar of some renown, a man famous for his calligraphy and poetry and who had a reputation as a fair minded judge. Neither of these men was related to either of the major contracting parties; the entire transaction took place with a cast of 'strangers.'

Existing ties of friendship are of paramount importance in facilitating the normal flow of social relationships in emergency. In Ch'uhsien the general population prefers to settle as many disputes as possible without recourse to the formal legal structure. As a matter of fact, such procedure had the implicit approval of the national political structure as stated in the legal code. At many points of law, courts were directed to adhere to local practice. Such a policy tends to reduce frictions which result when a generalized and impersonal code is applied to a specific locality. Thus in the Civil Code of the Republic of China there are frequent uses of the formula, " . . . if . . . otherwise provided for by custom, such custom shall be followed." [38] In the Agrarian Law of the People's Republic of China, adopted on June 28, 1950, there is also recourse to a similar slogan. Thus, in ordering the redistribution of irrigation rights, the Agrarian Law states, "If it is not convenient to distribute [the dam and pond rights], they should be democratically managed by the local people's government in conformity with established customs." [39]

[38] Civil Code of China, 1930-31, Articles 776, 778, 781, pp. 199-200; Articles 838 and 846, pp. 216-17.
[39] Agrarian Law of the People's Republic of China, 1950, Sect. IV, Article 17. See also: Sect. IV, Article 16; Article 23.

In actual practice, there are three ways of dealing with a civil suit. The first is the "appeal to affection" wherein the parties are exhorted to settle their difference amicably on the basis of the *kan-ch'ing* which exists between them. Most minor or petty issues are approached on this level, for example, the precise agreement over rice rentals between landlord and tenant, the fixing of the amount of arrears of a debtor, or a clash over responsibility for small accidents. If the issue cannot be settled on this basis, the second appeal is to "reason." Unlike the appeal to affection, the appeal to reason requires a mediator and provides one of the primary fields in which a gentleman validates his *kan-ch'ing* relationship with a peasant or tenant. The mediator is supposed to be a "gentleman" of recognized character who is not related to either party. Should some relationship be traceable, either through blood or functional connection (*i.e.*: landlord-tenant) the success of the mediation is likely to be undermined and a third party sought. Actually, the middleman-judges in these cases are not single persons, but are many in number. One is considered the chief mediator. It is his function to investigate the case and then circulate among his gentlemen friends, describing the case and soliciting opinions. When a body of agreement has been reached, the chief mediator announces the decision to the two parties. Most settlements are, in effect, compromises and are generally accepted with a minimum of fuss. The third possibility is least desirable and remains a last resort, to be used when the previous methods have failed to produce a settlement. After appeals to affection and reason have proven sterile the plaintiff takes his case into the civil court which is represented periodically at Ch'u by a circuit judge. Since such a procedure will involve lawyers and since it is certain that the affairs of both parties will come under the scrutiny of a remote and unknown third party, such a course is anathema for the average citizen and few are brought to this stage.

One case in point may illustrate much of the foregoing. In January, 1948, a tenant farmer who was conferring with a landlord was accidentally shot and killed by a servant of the landlord who was playing with the rifle of a soldier quartered in the landlord's house. Both the servant and the soldier, whose gun it was, were immediately imprisoned. Their fates were considered matters that concerned the civilian criminal authorities and the military police, respectively, and each malefactor was to be tried by the proper authority. As things developed, the soldier was acquitted with a warning against negligence and the servant drew a light sentence for manslaughter after it was established that the entire affair was simply a dreadful accident. The family of the dead man, however, was less interested in the criminal proceedings than in the question of compensation for its loss. Cutting to the heart of the matter, they claimed that eventual responsibility was the landlord's since the servant was only his instrument. An indemnity of CNC$20 million (about US$125.—) was asked. The landlord had already been cleared of legal responsibility by the formal political structure but conversations with influential gentlemen soon established the fact that general opinion held that the landlord had partial responsibility, a responsibility that could be met by the payment of an indemnity. The tenant farmer's family was not represented in the matter after its demands were stated, but the landlord himself solicited opinion. Finally, he announced that he would pay the family half of their original demand. His generosity was commended and the bond between himself and the tenant family was considered stronger than ever.

FAMILISM AND OFFICIALDOM

Before passing to a discussion of the place of the officials in the culture in terms of the analysis which is here being undertaken, it is necessary to justify the separation of the officials from the gentry whom we have already discussed at some length. The proper delineation of this problem requires treatment almost as lengthy as the investigation upon which we have already embarked. Therefore, at this point, we offer only a brief exposition. There is, unfortunately, much confusion between published statements on this point. Much of it stems from that classical starting point in the investigation of Chinese class—the estimate which is explicit in the culture itself. The classical view of Chinese classes organizes the population into four recognized groups and one which is *declassé*. The four groups in the order of recognized status are: the scholars, the farmers, the artisans, and the merchants. The out-class group is diversely populated with criminals and those involved in despised occupations. The classical view of Chinese class is of only limited use as a tool in the analysis of Chinese social structure. For example, one might ask, what is the effective participation in society of the various grades and ranks of soldiers who normally are lumped together and discarded as inferior?[39a] Likewise, in the analysis of the officialdom, is it not true that the great bulk

---

[39a] For a more extensive treatment of this problem see Fried, 1952, 1952a.

of officials take their origin from the gentry? Fei says that " . . . the gentry, being a class of people living on privileges, are anxious to enter officialdom," [40] but in a culture which sees officialdom as a frequent synonym for wealth and prestige, the criterion might be applied to the entire population. Taking another tack, the positions which make one an official are many and have different bureaucratic weights. In classical China the official was a man who had received his appointment after successfully completing a series of examinations. There were many official jobs which required no such preparation. Such positions included lowly assignments as yamen servants and runners who, at certain times, were even classified, because of their occupations, in out-class groups. Today, with the disappearance of the examination system, the line has become even more obscure. One says, for example, that the county magistrate is an official but his aide is not; the police-chief is an official but the policeman is not.

On the simplest level, it may be recognized that the number of persons in Ch'uhsien who qualify as officials is only a fraction of those who are included in the gentry. On the other hand, there are various officials whose origins are recognizably not of a gentry nature. There are some whose continued allegiance and identification is with such groups as the merchant or the artisan. The statement of Francis Hsu, that: "The facts given . . . may prove what by our definition they are supposed to prove, namely, that prominence (as officials) did not last over two or three generations in the vast majority of families." [41] is not

---

[40] Fei, 1946, p. 8.
[41] Hsu, 1948, pp. 305.

taken seriously by Hsu himself, and, when such statements are modified by Fei's claim that Chinese officials "abhor public duty," [42] almost total confusion results. It is not the purpose of the present paper to investigate these matters. It is sufficient for our own investigation to point out some of the obvious differences between the status "gentry" and the status "officialdom." Though the similarities between the gentry and the officials in the matter of kin ties and non-kin ties outweigh the discrepencies, nevertheless, it will be seen that certain new areas of social activity apply only to the present category.

Fei Hsiao-tung, after correctly diagnosing the tendency of the gentry to seek reinforcing positions in officialdom, makes a claim which seems incomplete to the point of serious error:

It is a recognized necessity for the rich to hold a position in the hierarchy. Clan organization and affinal confederation are sufficient because they are systems of security through the establishment of a relation to the power hierarchy by kinship.[43]

In any society in which the population is so huge as in China, even before the enormous increases of the Ch'ing period,[44] the thought of effective connection through kinship is unrealistic. The data from contemporary Ch'u indicate that much of the favorable connection between officials and others is based on non-kin types of social relationship. Even in the event of connection through kinship

---

[42] Fei, 1946, p. 9.
[43] Fei, 1946, p. 8. (Is it possible that Fei was misprinted in the original source?)
[44] Chen, Ta, 1946, p. 3.

of all gentry families with the power structure, there would be a serious lack of liaison and functional connection among the various officials, unless there were also amalgamating ties which by-passed kinship. Kin ties are not the main binding force in the society of Ch'uhsien. It is even less likely that they are a major force in Chinese society at large, a generalization that may well apply to the part two millenia of Chinese history, as well as the present.

It is true, however, that kinship is *one* of the preferred methods by which a gentry family may properly arrange its relationships with the power structure. We have already seen how connections of blood are used to ameliorate tax demands, and how the proper mention of the name of a well connected relative may spare one the indignities of quartering troops. But it is also possible and common to employ other types of ties in the place of kinship. For example, we may cite again the role of the magistrate's secretary among his friends. The secretary, in his own career, gives an illustration of the importance of non-kin ties in politics. The secretary of the magistrate was also his *protégé,* but the two men had met in the provincial capital where the magistrate had been employed in a bureau which the secretary entered as a lowly appointee. Despite a difference in age of more than fifteen years, a friendship developed. When the magistrate was appointed to Ch'-uhsien, he brought his friend with him. Actually, the magistrate had three secretaries. One was his young friend, one was an older friend who was skilled in political manipulation and whose primary job was to shield the magistrate from the public. The third secretary was a relative who held a sinecure and who spent less time in Ch'u than he did in his home district.

Ch'u had two major political groups. They were not 'parties' since they were not organized and had no extensive general memberships. Actually, they were cliques led by individuals of great local prominence. One group was headed by the aged father of a prominent official in the Nationalist government; the other was headed by a retired general. The rivalry between the groups was friendly and the leaders were on excellent terms. A sample problem and its solution will show how these groups, despite a relative lack of cross-cutting kinship ties, managed to operate so smoothly, that conflict was minimized and the involvement of the general populace was avoided.

The issue was the appointment of a representative to the National Assembly, which was to elect a national president and vice-president. Also at stake was the election of the head of the local Peoples' Political Council. On one side, the local candidates were the national official and his father; on the other, the general and a friend named "C". For a time, it seemed that the solution could be found only after a knockdown drag-out political battle. Nothing could be farther from actuality.

Three things modified the conditions which were stated. The general had a son whose ambition was to study in a medical school in the United States. The father of the national official was an old man whose last desire was to be head of the P.P.C. Last, in a way that never became clear to the writer, there was an open seat in the Judicial Yuan in Nanking which was controlled by the national official. Under these circumstances, meetings began, generally taking place in the friendly atmosphere of a private house, over the wine cups in a restaurant and, as I heard, in Nanking. When the solution appeared it took shape in the form of action rather than as a statement or prediction.

It became understood that the general's son had been very fortunate and would soon leave to study medicine in the United States. Mr. C. quietly announced his appointment to the Judicial Yuan and left the local race. The father of the national official was elected head of the P.P.C. and appointed his son delegate to the National Assembly. After a few months, the old man retired with his ambition fulfilled; the office passed to the retired general. Everybody had been served.

In the settlement of such a high level political problem of Ch'u, it is evident that certain family ties were involved. These kin ties operated, for the most part, only in the provision of basic alignments. Beyond that, kinship was of little moment. Most of the action took place along lines determined by friendship and the distribution of power. In the account given, the event was simplified. Actually, most of the persons in the power structure of Ch'u, the big merchants and wealthy landlords, as well as the major local officials, all were engaged in the manoeuvers and figured in the solution. When the whole panorama of a single involved political action is studied, the elements in it which are kin derived shrink in importance, while the non-kin factors swell accordingly. Thus, the tie between both political groups and the magistrate is one of the shared interest plus *kan-ch'ing;* kinship only appears in an indirect way, namely, that each side through kinship and friendship can point to some outside power which is greater than the magistrate and can claim that power as ally. The magistrate himself, in classical China, was not even a native of the province in which he operated, much less the county, since the "law of avoidance" assured his assignments to a distant place.[45] Actually, the positions of underclerks were often of great power and attempts might be made to conciliate them. At any rate, as a recent commentator on the government of Nationalist China has written,

. . . . in general, there has been no real self government for the *hsien*. The *hsien* authorities have been as much the agents of the provincial government as the provincial ones are those of the central government.[46]

The quest for the source of ultimate authority and power in Chinese local government is not our proper subject, but the fact that such an inquiry immediately leads one beyond the range of the family and effective kinship ties is of great significance.

---

[45] Hsieh Pao-chao, 1925, p. 306.
[46] Ch'ien, 1950, p. 227.

extra-familial relationships in ch'uhsien

It is apparent that the citizen of all classes in Ch'uhsien lives much of his life beyond the orbit of relationships provided either by his family or the kinship system in which he is involved. On the basis of field data, we have concluded that most of the extra-kin contacts and associations do not repeat familistic organization or familial functions. Instead, there is a complete and well developed realm of non-familial contacts in Ch'uhsien which, independent of kin connections, may on occasion compete with kinship ties for the basic loyalty of the individual. On most occasions, however, extra-kin relationships complement pre-existing ties of conjugal or affinal kinship.

APPLICATION OF NON-KIN TIES

All elements of the population, rich and poor, rural and urban, peasant and gentry, engage in extensive non-kin relationships. The fields in which these relationships take place are numerous and diverse. No Chinese family of my acquaintanceship is, to any significant degree, self-sufficient. The poorest elements in the Chinese population,

the beggars, are not only completely dependent upon outside society for their subsistence, but are frequently organized as a body, for the sake of increased efficiency.
Likewise, the richest and most stable gentry families are
attached to a myriad non-related individuals. Some of
these supply the rich family its subsistence, others aid it
in the defense of its position.

The areas in which extra-kin activity takes place are diverse and cover almost the entire range of human experience. Within this broad field, however, certain areas show
particular importance. The first of such areas is the economic. In the disposition of excess labor, for example, the
peasantry comes face to face with a fundamental problem
of subsistence which is only in small part a kin matter.
Its solution inevitably carries into fields beyond those of
kinship.

When peaceful actions fail to solve peasant problems,
as for example in this case, the process of labor distribution through periodic migration or emigration, there
comes another phenomenon which has frequently dominated the historical scene. Rebellion, which sees hordes of
unrelated persons acting together in concert with the goal
of revising the *status quo,* has been common in China.
The basic process has been aptly described:

It is quite natural that the common tendency among the
peasants is not to rise on the social ladder but rather to sink
toward the bottom. A petty owner may become a tenant when
he sells his land as misfortune befalls him. He may further
sink from a tenant to a landless farm laborer. He may in the
end die disgracefully or disappear from the village. These outcasts are desperate. They have nothing to lose but their life of
drudgery. They leave the village and plunge themselves into

banditry or smuggling, or join the army, or seek employment as servants in big gentry houses. These are economically unproductive jobs, but it is only by taking such jobs, in addition to good luck, that the outcasts from the rural society can hope to obtain wealth quickly. Of course, hundreds and thousands of such outcasts die in despair and are forgotten by the world. They are the dissatisfied class and thus revolutionary in nature. When the ruling class is strong they are suppressed. Only a few reach their aim through various kinds of more or less unlawful ways. But if the ruling class is degenerate and weak, they are the uprising group aiming at power. In Chinese history there are several instances where new dynasties were inaugurated by such desperate outcasts.[1]

It is evident that Chinese society is not based on a simple, tribal type of economy in which the population uniformly repeats a small number of processes in their quest for livelihood. An explanation in terms of simple reciprocity is also out of the question. China is involved in a money economy. Even the slaves of such a classical age as the Han could own and deal in currency.[2] The urban and rural populations of China alike use money in the pursuit of subsistence and profit. Money even circulates within the family and may be the shoal upon which the ship of family unity founders.

Chinese economy is based upon an elaborate division of labor. Many specialties and a number of levels of wealth and control of production are involved. The framework upon which this system is articulated is not a kin system but a civil society. At times the civil power has been rigidly policed. At other times it has been internally

---

[1] Fei, 1946, pp. 10-11.
[2] Wilbur, 1943, pp. 219-220.

rent to such an extent that the countryside has witnessed general outbreaks of violence and rebellion.

Within the political arena, the balance of police forces and rebellious masses presents a strategic point at which non-kin forces interact. It has been shown that few, if any, families or groupings of extended kin can operate for long in the social milieu of Ch'uhsien without making contact with some powerful agency of legal enforcement, exploitation, or generalized control. That such has been the fact in Chinese society, historically, seems evident. China has known centralized state organization for more than two thousand years, and had a feudal organization for a millennium before that.

The government of China has long had a sophisticated tradition of centralized authority and power. It is true, as has been shown in a local context, that attempts are made to conciliate the power of the state by seeking to establish relationships with the power structure through the reckoning of kinship ties. Unfortunately, it is this aspect of Chinese political organization which too often has been stressed. Laments over the enervating effects of nepotism in bureaucracy are frequent in the literature but *kanch'ing,* friendship, and neighborhood are also important forces in the alignment of political and economic power. In certain cases, as has been shown, those factors may rank well above kinship in the assignment of political roles and powers.

It is not only in the fields of economics and politics that the effects of non-kin ties are apparent. The Chinese ceremonial systems are largely based on familial ties which ramify through extended kin groupings but which finally emerge into a world of non-kin relationships. We note at this point the purchase of religious and ceremonial artifacts from non-kin sources and the general lack of kin ties with the professional religious functionaries. We note also that the attendance and participation of non-related individuals in religious events may be of central importance in the rituals. In many instances, religious affairs are combined with other aspects of life in the field of ceremonial. Often such a combination casts light on some significant dependent relationship that exceeds the kinship system. Thus, the role sometimes played by an important official in the encoffining of the dead combines sanctioned funeral beliefs and a method of dealing with and encouraging relationships with non-related officialdom.

Self-sufficiency in any major area of daily life is almost totally absent in Ch'uhsien. One apparent exception is in the field of education within certain specialized groups. Thus the hired agricultural worker learns little beyond the materials supplied by familial contacts. Even this however, does not stand up in detail. The child of such a worker profits from his contacts with outsiders even though these contacts may be few when compared with those of an urban child. Nor does such an individual fail to continue his education when he becomes adult. The tomato entered Ch'u gardening largely through the observations which were made by a hired garden worker in the experimental farm of Nanking University. He convinced a relative of his, a tenant gardener in Ch'u, that the plant was worthy of trial and supplied him with seed. The mere exposure of the rural workman to varied conditions expands his knowledge in ways that would not be possible if he remained within the narrow compass of his family.

NON-KIN TIES: AN ANALYSIS

The data on non-kin ties in Ch'uhsien show two major types of polarization. First, a rural-urban division is evident; second, some class alignments are obvious. In the rural sphere, momentarily disregarding class divisions, the most pressing problems are those of subsistence, the maintenance of production, and the disposal of surplus labor. The decisive factor is the agricultural milieu itself, from which these factors may not be separated lest they become meaningless. Thus, certain facts: that seed is also food, the weather is beyond control, different seasons require different labor budgets, etc., may not be separated from the fact that a poor season may see the consumption of capital as food, that a drought may send one to the usurers, or that extra sons will overtax the resources of the farm. From such comparisons we may conclude that, although there are many superficial resemblances between rural and urban problems, seen as abstractions, such similarities often exceed the functional reality of the underlying situation.

One element in the rural population seems strangely out of place. The rural gentry are distinct only by virtue of location in the countryside. Their affiliations, functions and techniques of operation are distinctly at odds with those of the vast majority of the rural population. Does this mean that two distinct and dissimilar types are equally normal products of rural areas? On the contrary, a comparison of the urban gentry and the rural gentry shows such unanimity of feeling and action that there can be no doubt that sociologically the rural gentry are displaced from their proper milieu. The final demonstration of this matter does not depend on reason; fortunately, there are a number of empirical facts which complement the logical analysis and offer proof of its validity. The rural gentry in Ch'uhsien has been steadily moving into the city over the past five decades and more. The movement is slow but continuous. The rural gentry located at any great remove from city walls finds itself in an increasingly hostile environment as civil controls are weakened. The kin ties of gentry families are inadequate and cannot effectively establish them in the bosom of a large and protective mass of people. Their functional position in the countryside hastens their removal. Their fundamental interests demand that they maintain their positions through the repeated extraction of local surpluses through the collection of rents, interest, and taxes. Emphasis on these functions can only circumscribe the development of friendships. The alternative to friendship is *kan-ch'ing* which, unlike friendship, not only recognizes exploitation but is a technique of ameliorating it. Even *kan-ch'ing*, however, requires more fertile social soil and the best the gentry can do is establish good *kan-ch'ing* with a few persons while relationships with others deteriorate.

Once again the most important symbol of the situation is the constant undercurrent of violence and rebellion which was mentioned above. The gentry in the country who are removed from the potential aid of the punitive military forces stationed in the ·cities, are the exposed victims of such bandit or sporadic rebellious activity as may take place in the locality. Under these conditions the gentry are spurred to move into the city, there to seek the physical protection of the walls and the social protection of such officials as may be approached through ties of kinship and *kan-ch'ing*.

Categories are never as clearcut in actuality as they can be made in description. The well-established peasant differs from the gentleman primarily in his actual occupation with the soil. The rich tenants sometimes take on functions of landlords, collecting rents on lands which they sublease. On the other hand, both wealthy peasants and well-to-do tenants frequently pretend to a standard living usually associated with the very poor, wearing ragged clothes and living in small, badly kept houses. The reasons for this are several and involve both practical and religious considerations. One of the major sources of this pattern, however, is in the field of non-kin relationships. The peasant or rich tenant cannot, like the rural gentry, leave the land and enter the city, because his livelihood is based on his continued presence and labor on a farm. Through usury or sub-leasing he may weaken the bonds of friendship or *kan-ch'ing*. His circle of relatives is even smaller than that of the gentry. His only defence is in dissimulation, and he pretends to a lower level of income in the hope of avoiding the attention of the bandits. In keeping with this, wealthy peasants in Ch'uhsien, which has always had an extraordinary predilection for banditry, have long preferred to invest their surpluses in the slow accumulation of private land. This process was upset in 1947-48 by the approach of the Communists when most wealthy peasants concentrated on building up a mobile surplus through investments in high interest bearing, short term loans.

TYPES OF NON-KIN TIES: A PROVISIONAL ANALYSIS

It is not possible, as yet, to correlate distinctive forms of non-kin relationships with various specific social levels.

It would be quite valuable for certain types of analysts, for example, personality and culture specialists, to know that certain types of friendships appear at certain places in the social structure, while certain types of *kan-ch'ing* have other correlations. While definite conclusions are not warranted by the data, certain generalizations may be hazarded.

Friendship, by which is meant a relationship between two or more persons based on mutual affection and sympathy and devoid of the object of exploitation, clearly exists on all levels of Ch'uhsien society. Tenant farmers, merchants, landlord-gentry, and artisans, even the beggars display deep and permanent friendly attachments. Though factors of personality are of utmost importance in determining the degree to which any given individual will seek to enlarge his circle of friends, it also seems as though the extent of that circle also depends on the position in society of the persons concerned. People of higher status tend to have more leisure time than lower ones. They also move in an urban, heavily populated milieu. Their education and interests are broader, hence they have a wider area of receptivity to new contacts. As a class they control more power functions than do the lower statuses, hence the cultivation of their friendship is more desirable.

Kan-ch'ing differs from friendship in that it presumes a much more specific common interest, much less warmth and more formality of contact, and includes a recognized degree of exploitation. It is the common property of all classes. We have stressed certain manifestations of *kan-ch'ing*, particularly those which are of aid in binding the landlord-tenant relationship. We have also reviewed the relationships which help gentlemen of lower status to stabilize their positions with regard to the power of the state. Both of these types of *kan-ch'ing*, as well as others, such as the relationship between master and apprentice, shop official and clerk, etc., have one thing in common: class lines are cross-cut; *kan-ch'ing* operates in the absence of kin ties which can bridge important gaps in status.

This last point has certain implications for a general comparative study of culture and raise questions for further research. Is *kan-ch'ing* merely one specific attempt in a particular culture to reconcile the personal contacts of a kin-organized society with the impersonal relationships which are demanded in all cultures which operate through a civil organization? Is *kan-ch'ing* functionally similar to the *compadre* relationship in Spanish-America, or medieval Europe? Before attempts are made to answer such queries, there will have to be more studies similar to this one, each with its focus in a different culture.

Certain specific types of non-kin association appear on certain levels but do not appear on others. The labor-sharing cooperative is clearly rural and applies to peasants and tenant-farmers. Not even among the urbanized gardeners does it appear. Likewise, the guild, which despite its formal establishment by the national government is the attempt of urban merchants and craftsmen to stabilize conditions and mediate with an impersonal and potentially dangerous power, does not appear, in a functionally comparable way, in the countryside. There is a Farmers' Guild in Ch'uhsien but, unlike the Merchant and Service Guilds, it has not arisen on the basis of any need felt by the farmers themselves. Instead, it was imposed, in its present form, from the outside by the Nationalist Government and was a technique of attempted control. The officers of the Farmers' Guild were all of gentry origin, almost all of them prominent absentee landlords. Most farmers in Ch'uhsien whom I had the opportunity of interviewing did not even know that there was such a guild and none could say what its purpose was.

There are many other specific associations which are limited to precise sectors of the social structure. Credit societies of many different types, various kinds of schools, and different kinds of religious associations have memberships which sometimes are generalized but which frequently are quite specially oriented to the needs of a specific element in the society. The data collected on many of these institutions are so thin and so lacking in functional depth that any approach to their meaning in the larger society must be largely conjectural.

KIN, NON-KIN AND CLASS IN CHINESE SOCIETY

In stating the above, the intention is not to limit unduly the conclusions of this study. It is still clear that such clan forces as exist in Ch'uhsien are vitally involved in the non-kin processes which have been described. Sometimes the relationship is a clear one.

An important clue to the situation, once again, is the prevalence of banditry and rebellion. Both of these forces operate at maximum efficiency where the ties of kinship, especially those ties of extended kinship, are weakened. Clearly, in the organization of a bandit group the basic ties are not those of kinship but those of mutual profit or some other non-kin principle. This is reflected in the oaths which are sworn in certain secret societies, among which are societies which have had revolutionary significance. Thus the members of a secret society may be forced to swear prior allegiance and loyalty to fellow members, even at the expense of their own fathers or brothers.

Observations made on banditry in Ch'uhsien confirm the importance of non-kin forces in the class orientation of a society. One day, a number of poorly dressed young men were pushed through the streets of the city, led to the South gate and there were shot. They were bandits who had been active in the county for several months. All were deserters from the Nationalist Army and they had made their livings for some time by raiding outlying settlements and robbing the rich peasants or the die-hard rural gentry. For several months they were successful and then, quite suddenly, they were caught. The explanation was simple. Several times a company of the local militia had been marched into the countryside to find the marauders but each time the bandits had vanished. During their early patrol, the guerrillas' efforts had been confined to the looting of more or less wealthy families. The general populace, not molested, was either apathetic or actively sympathetic to the bandits. Then, for reasons unknown, the bandits failed to discriminate and began raids on ordinary peasants and tenant villagers, often burning the houses of their victims. Unconcern immediately became active interest. The peasantry kept tabs on the location of the bandits and informed the local authorities. A company of Nationalist troops was alerted. Finally, this company was led to the exact place in which the bandits were hiding and the rebels were destroyed. The interpretation of such events calls clearly for the recognition of non-kin forces on both sides, and, what is more, a recognition of the fact that those non-kin forces tend to be patterned in some way along class lines.

One last remark on class orientations seems necessary. The rural tenants and workers would seem to be logically related to the urban workers and, indeed, there are many points held in common. Yet there are many dissimilarities in regard to the nature of their extra-kin dependence. The community of action between these two groups has never been high, even in the recent revolutionary situation. There are many individuals who have moved from one group into the other and thereby transferred loyalties and adopted new modes of behavior, but the occurrence of a simple feeling of identity transcending the obvious differences of location and precise specialization and concentration on the similar relationship to the techniques of production has, as yet, not been realized.

The complex design of Chinese society becomes more comprehensible when systematic study of extra-familial relations is added to the research on Chinese familial organization. Non-kin forces are diverse. They ramify through the entire social structure and furnish the links between kin-based activity and movements in the larger civil areas of society.

To a certain degree, non-kin mechanisms complement kin relationships. Many such ties are entered into for the purpose of nourishing or defending close relatives— a wife, parents, or children. Often kinship relations, rendered increasingly feeble by the encroachment of the civil apparatus, must be reinforced, and so it is that such institutions as that of *kan-ch'ing,* normally operative in the non-kin field, are extended to strengthen ties between relatives. Likewise, friendships may supplement well-founded and satisfactory emotional situations in the family, supplying added elements of novelty and appeal. Sometimes, however, non-kin forces oppose kin ties. Ambivalence may arise over the nexus of primary loyalty. Should the merchant employ a relative or a friend—or a highly skilled stranger? Shall one side with friends whose interests and opinions mirror one's one or shall one adhere to family ways——old ways? These questions, seemingly innocuous when phrased as sociological abstractions, become burning questions of the day in a society in upheaval. Revolutionary movements frequently demand behavior which conflicts with the codes of kinship groups. The present situation in China, where the strength of the Communist government rests largely on the fervid support and loyalty of the youth of the nation, gives proof of this. Furthermore, the success of the Chinese Communist Party in this regard may be most clearly understood when viewed against the backdrop of a study of the pre-existing extra-kin mechanisms in Chinese society. For, as I have shown, the basic production of subsistence, ceremonial, and religious goods and the satisfaction of fundamental needs for education and recreation, continually exceeds the sphere of familial capacity.

This is not a Chinese problem alone. The determination of the points at which kin-based action is superceded by non-kin and then by civil action is a cultural problem *par excellence*. The revolt of the colonial areas of the world, perhaps the most significant political movement of our century, appears when the early kin basis of the society is thoroughly smashed and non-kin associations rise to the fore. When more studies have been made in many different societies, a truly broad, comparative and systematic analysis of the operation of civil society will become possible. Then we will better understand the formation of nationalities and the nature of class loyalties. We will be in a suitable scientific position to return to a major and unfulfilled question of nineteenth century social science, the nature of the evolution of human society.

THE END

bibliography

I. BOOKS AND ARTICLES CITED DIRECTLY IN TEXT

"Agrarian Law of the People's Republic of China," 1950, Supplement to *People's China*, II, No. 2.

Biggerstaff, Knight, 1940, "The Peasant Family: The Chinese Large Family, its Role and Recent Trends," *The Cultural Approach to History*, C. F. Ware (ed.), Columbia University Press, New York.

Buck, J. L., 1930, *Chinese Farm Economy*, University of Chicago Press, Chicago.

——, 1937, *Land Utilization in China*, 3 vol., University of Chicago Press, Chicago.

Burgess, J. S., 1928, *The Guilds of Peking*, Columbia University Press, New York.

Chang, C. M., 1936, "Tax Farming in North China: A Case Study of the System of Auctioned Revenue Collections made in Ching-hai Hsien, Hopei Province," *Nankai Social and Economic Quarterly*, VIII, No. 4.

Chang Ch'eng-k'un, 1939, "The Chinese Large Family System and Its Disorganization," *Social Forces*, XVII.

Chao Ch'eng-hsin, 1948, "P'ing Chiao Tsun as a Social Laboratory," *Yenching Journal of Social Studies*, IV, No. 1.

Chen Han-seng, 1936, *Landlord and Peasant in China*, International Publishers, New York.

Chen Ta, 1940, *Emigrant Communities in South China*, Institute of Pacific Relations, New York.

————, 1946, *Population in Modern China,* University of Chicago Press, Chicago.

————, 1947, "Basic Problems of the Chinese Working Class," *American Journal of Sociology,* LIII, No. 3.

Cheng Lin-chuang, 1937, "The Kao-tsi Railway Consumers' Cooperative," *Yenching Journal of Social Studies,* I, No. 1.

Chiang Mon-lin, 1945, *Tides From the West,* Yale University Press, New Haven.

Ch'ien Tuan-sheng, 1950, *The Government and the Politics of China,* Harvard University Press, Cambridge.

Civil Code of the Republic of China, 1930-31, 2 vols., Hsia, Chow and Chang (trans.) , Shanghai.

De Groot, J. J. M., 1892-1913, *The Religious System of China,* 6 vols., E. J. Brill, Leyden.

"Decisions Concerning the Differentiation of Class Status in the Countryside," 1950, *People's China,* Supplement to Vol. 2, No. 8.

Djang, Y. S., 1931, "Credit Cooperatives in 1,000 Villages," *Chinese Social and Political Science Review,* XV.

Durkheim, E., 1933, *The Division of Labor in Society,* George Simpson (trans.) , The Macmillan Company, New York.

Favre, B., 1933, *Les Sociétés Secrètes en Chine,* Maison-neuve, Paris.

Fei Hsiao-tung, 1939, *Peasant Life in China,* G. Routledge & Sons, Ltd., London.

————, 1941, "Agricultural Labor in a Yunnan Village," *Nankai Social and Economic Quarterly,* XII, Nos. 1-2.

————, 1946, "Peasantry and Gentry in China," *American Journal of Sociology,* LII, No. 1.

————, 1948, "Problems of Rural Industrialization," *China Economist,* I, No. 4.

Fei Hsiao-tung and Chang Chih-I, 1945, *Earthbound China,* University of Chicago Press, Chicago.

Fitzgerald, C. P., 1941, *The Tower of Five Glories,* The Cresset Press, London.

Fong, H. D., 1937, "Industrial Organization in China," *Nankai Social and Economic Quarterly,* IX, No. 4.

Fried, M. H., 1949, "Some Preliminary Considerations of Larger Units in Chinese Social Organization," *Transactions of the New York Academy of Sciences,* Ser. II, Vol. 11, No. 4.

————, 1952, "Military Status in Chinese Society," *American Journal of Sociology,* LVII.

————, 1952a, "Chinese Society: Class as Subculture," *Transaction of the New York Academy of Sciences,* Ser. II, Vol. 14, No. 8

Hommel, Rudolf, 1937, *China at Work,* Doylestown, Pa.

Hsieh Pao-chao, 1925, *The Government of China,* (1644-1911) , Johns Hopkins University Press, Baltimore.

Hsieh Ping-ying, 1940, *Autobiography of a Girl Rebel,* John Day Company, New York.

Hsu, Francis L. K., 1943, "The Myth of Chinese Family Size," *American Journal of Sociology,* XLVIII, No. 5.

———, 1945a, *Magic, Science and Religion in Yunnan,* Institute of Pacific Relations, New York.

———, 1945b, "Observations on Cross Cousin Marriage in China," *American Anthropologist,* 47:1.

———, 1948, *Under the Ancestors' Shadow,* Columbia University Press, New York.

———, 1949a, "The Chinese Family," *The Family, Its Functions and Destiny,* R. Anshen (ed.) , Harcourt, Brace and Co., New York.

———, 1949b, "China," in *Most of the World,* R. Linton (ed.), Columbia University Press, New York.

Hu Hsien-chin, 1948, *The Common Descent Group in China and Its Functions,* The Viking Fund Publications in Anthropology, No. 10, New York.

Institute of Pacific Relations, 1939, *Agrarian China,* R. H. Tawney (ed.) , New York.

Kulp, D. H., 1925, *Country Life in South China,* Teachers College, Columbia University Bureau of Publications, New York.

———, 1930, "Chinese Continuity," *Annals of the American Academy of Political and Social Science,* CLII.

Lang, Olga, 1946, *Chinese Family and Society,* Yale University Press, New Haven.

Lattimore, Owen, 1950, *Pivot of Asia,* Atlantic, Brown & Co., Boston.

Lau Shaw, 1945, *Ricksha Boy,* Evans King (trans.), Reynal, Hitchcock & Company, New York.

———, 1948, *The Quest for Love of Lao Lee,* Helena Kuo (trans.) , Reynal, Hitchcock & Company, New York.

Lee, F. C. H., and T. Chin, 1929, *Village Families in the Vicinity of Peiping,* Bulletin of the Institute of Social Research, No. 2.

Legge, James, 1861, *The Confucian Analects, the Great Learning and the Doctrine of the Mean,* Trubner & Co., London.

———, 1871, *The She King,* Trubner & Company, London.

Levy, Marion J., 1949, *The Family Revolution in Modern China,* Harvard University Press, Cambridge.

Levy, M. J. and Shih Kuo-heng, 1949, *The Rise of the Modern Chinese Business Class,* Institute of Pacific Relations, New York.

Liao T'ai-ch'u, 1948, "The Apprentices in Chengtu During and After the War," *Yenching Journal of Social Studies,* IV, No. 1.

Lin Yutang, 1947, *The Gay Genius,* John Day Co., New York.

Lin Yueh-hwa, 1947, *The Golden Wing,* Institute of Pacific Relations, New York.

Lowie, R. H., 1948, *Social Organization,* New York.

Malinowski, B., 1926, *Crime and Custom in Savage Society*, The Macmillan Company, New York.

Morse, Hosea Ballou, 1909, *The Gilds of China*, Longmans, London.

Murdock, G. P., 1949, *Social Structure*, The Macmillan Company, New York.

Opler, Morris E., 1950, "Review of G. P. Murdock's *Social Structure*," *American Anthropologist*, LII.

Playfair, G. M. H., 1879, *The Cities and Towns of China: a Geographical Dictionary*, Noronha, Hongkong.

Pruitt, Ida, 1945, *Daughter of Han*, Yale University Press, New Haven.

Schlegel, Gustave, 1866, *Thian Ti Hwui, The Hung League*, Lange, Batavia.

Stanton, William, 1900, *The Triad Society*, Kelly & Walsh, Hongkong.

Steward, J. H., 1950, *Area Research, Theory and Practice*, Social Science Research Council, Bulletin 63, New York.

Su Sing-ging, 1922, *The Chinese Family System*, International Publishers, New York.

Tang Chi-yu, 1924, *An Economic Study of Chinese Agriculture*, Cornell, Ithaca, New York.

Tao and Leong, 1915, *Village and Town Life in China*, G. Allen and Unwin, London.

Tawney, R. H., 1932, *Land and Labour in China*, G. Allen and Unwin, London.

Tsu Yu-yue, 1912, *The Spirit of Chinese Philanthropy*, Columbia University Press, New York.

Ward, J. S. and W. G. Stirling, 1927, *The Hung Society or the Society of Heaven and Earth*, 3 vols., The Baskerville Press, London.

Warner, W. L., M. Meeker and K. Eels, 1949, *Social Class in America*, University of Chicago Press, Chicago.

Wilbur, C. M., 1933, *Village Government in China*, unpublished Master's essay, Columbia University.

————, 1943, *Slavery in China During the Former Han Dynasty, 206 B.C.- A.D. 25*, Field Museum of Natural History, Anthropology Series, No. 34, Chicago.

Wu Hwa-pao, 1936, "Agricultural Economy of Yung-lo Hsien in Shensi Province," *Nankai Social and Economic Quarterly*, IX, No. 1.

Wu Yuey-len, 1936, "The Boat People of Shanam: A Statistical Study of Population and Economic Conditions," *Nankai Social and Economic Quarterly*, IX, No. 3.

Yang, H. K., 1937, "The Cooperative Movement in China," *Bulletin of the Central Bank of China*, III, No. 2.

Yang, Martin, 1945, *A Chinese Village*, Columbia University Press, New York.

II. SUPPLEMENTARY BIBLIOGRAPHY

Bucklin, H. S., 1924, *A Social Survey of Sung-Ka-Hong, China,* Brown-in-China, Monograph No. 1, Shanghai.

Chao Ch'eng-hsin, 1940, "Familism as a Factor in the Chinese Population Balance," *Yenching Journal of Social Studies,* II, No. 1.

Chen, T. S. and J. Shyrock, 1932, "Chinese Relationship Terms," *American Anthropologist,* XXXIV.

Chu, T. S. and T. Chin, 1929, *Marketing of Cotton in Hopei Province,* Bulletin of the Institute of Social Research, No. 3.

Courant, Maurice, 1899, "Les Associations en Chine," *Annales des Sciences Politiques,* XIV.

Dickenson, Jean, 1924, *Observations on the Social Life of a North China Village,* Yenching University, Department of Sociology, Series C, No. 6, Peiping.

Emerson, Mills and Thompson, 1942, *Government and Nationalism in Southeast Asia,* Institute of Pacific Relations, New York.

Fairbank, J. K., 1948, *The United States and China,* Harvard University Press, Cambridge.

Fei Hsiao-tung, 1936-37, "The Problem of Chinese Relationship System," *Monumenta Serica,* XX.

Feng Han-yi, 1937, "The Chinese Kinship System," *Harvard Journal of Asiatic Studies,* II, No. 2.

Fong, H. D., 1935, "Rural Weaving and the Merchant Employers in a North China District," *Nankai Social and Economic Quarterly,* 8, No. 4.

Fong, H. D., and Y. T. Ku, 1934-35, "Shoe Making in a North China Port," *Chinese Social and Political Science Review,* XVIII.

Hahn, Clarence C., 1928, "Psycho-social Effects of the Chinese Family System," *Sociology and Social Research,* XII, No. 5.

Highbaugh, Irma, 1948, *Family Life in West China,* Agricultural Mission, New York.

Hsu Chi-Lien, 1928, "Rural Credit in China," *Chinese Social and Political Science Review,* XII.

Hsu, F. L. K. and J. H. Hu, 1945, "Guild and Kinship among the Butchers in West Town," *American Sociological Review,* vol. 10.

Hsu, L. S., 1933, *Study of a Typical Chinese Town,* Yenching University, Department of Sociology and Social Work, Series C, No. 26.

Hsu, P. C., 1929, "Rural Cooperatives in China," *Pacific Affairs,* II.

Kiang Wen-han, 1948, *The Chinese Student Movement,* King's Crown Press, New York.

Kroeber, A. L., 1932, "Process in the Chinese Kinship System," *American Anthropologist,* XXXV.

Lee, Rose Hum, 1949, "Research on the Chinese Family," *American Journal of Sociology,* LIV, No. 6.

Li An-che, 1938, "Notes on the Necessity of Field Research in Social Science in China," *Yenching Journal of Social Studies*, I.

Mallory, W. H., 1931, "Rural Cooperative Credit in China," *The Quarterly Journal of Economics*, XXXXV.

Maybon, Pierre B., 1925, *Essai sur les Associations en Chine*, Plon-Hourrit, Paris.

Ruh Tsuin Ts'ui, 1940, "Farm Management Study of Eight Representative Localities in North China," *The Chinese Social and Political Science Review*, XXIV, No. 3.

Shih Kuo-heng, 1944, *China Enters the Machine Age*, Harvard University Press, Cambridge.

Smith, Arthur H., 1899, *Village Life in China*, F. H. Revell Co., New York.

Tao, L. K., 1934, "Some Chinese Characteristics in the Light of the Chinese Family," *Essays Presented to C. G. Seligman*, Kegan Paul, Trench, Trubner & Co., London.

Taylor, J. B., 1937-38, "The Co-operative Movement in China," *Chinese Social and Political Science Review*, XXI, No. 1.

Werner, E. T. C., 1919, *China and the Chinese*, Pitman, London.

Wilkinson, H. B., 1926, *The Family in Classical China*, Kelly & Walsh, Shanghai.

Wittfogel, K. A., 1938, *New Light on Chinese Society*, Institute of Pacific Relations, New York.

Wu Chih, 1934, "Handloom Weaving in Kaoyang," *Monthly Bulletin on Economic China*, VII, No. 6.

Wu Yuey-len, 1937, "Life and Culture of the Shanam Boat People," *Nankai Social and Economic Quarterly*, IX, No. 4.

Yen Ching-yueh, 1934, "Crime in Relation to Social Change in China," *American Journal of Sociology*, XL.

Yenching University, 1931, *Ching Ho, the Report of the Preliminary Survey of the Town of Ching Ho, Hopei, North China*.

Zen, Sophia H. Chen (ed.), 1931, *Symposium on Chinese Culture*, China Institute of Pacific Relations.

appendix

SPECIALIZATIONS IN CH'U

I. Specializations recognized by inclusion within the combined Service Guild as separate bodies.

1. Painters, masons and carpenters
2. Porters and coffin carriers
3. Wheelbarrow men
4. Cigarette makers
5. Barbers
6. Basketmakers
7. Beancurd makers
8. Hotel personnel
9. Tailors
10. Cotton ginners
11. Noodle (and processed wheat products) makers
12. Leather tanners
13. Ricksha men
14. Restaurant waiters and bath-house attendants
15. Water sellers
16. Blacksmiths
17. Tinsmiths
18. Fuel grass jobbers

19. Candy makers and bakers
20. Charcoal jobbers
21. Firecracker makers
22. Incense and candle makers
23. Pole carriers
24. Truck farmers
25. Rice polishers

II. Specializations recognized by inclusion within the combined Commercial Guild as separate bodies.
   1. Grain exchanges
   2. Cloth shops
   3. "Groceries"
   4. Import goods stores
   5. "Yang" stores (see p. 26)
   6. Eating oils stores
   7. Herb stores
   8. Lumber yards
   9. Restaurants
   10. Pottery shops
   11. Tea stores
   12. Hotels and bath-houses
   13. Transport firms
   14. Fruit stores
   15. Livestock commission merchants
   16. Slaughter houses and butcher shops
   17. Incense and candle stores
   18. Salt stores
   19. Other (i.e., jewelry, sign shop, gold exchange, etc.)

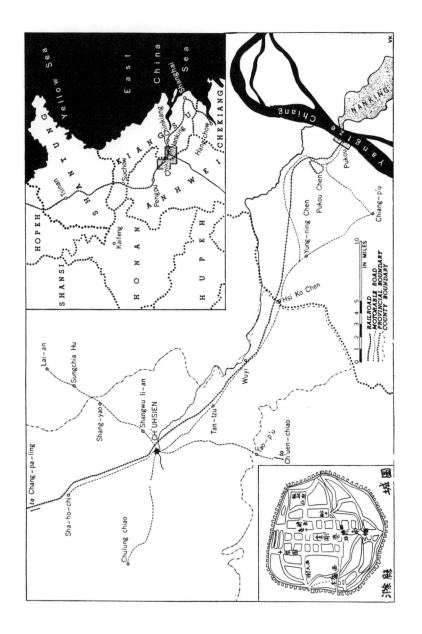

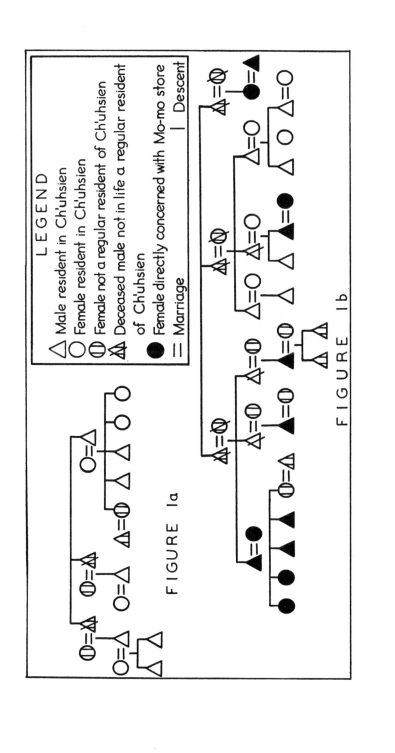

LEGEND

△ Male resident in Ch'uhsien

○ Female resident in Ch'uhsien

⬭ Female not a regular resident of Ch'uhsien

◮ Deceased male not in life a regular resident of Ch'uhsien

● Female directly concerned with Mo-mo store

= Marriage

| Descent

FIGURE 1a

FIGURE 1b

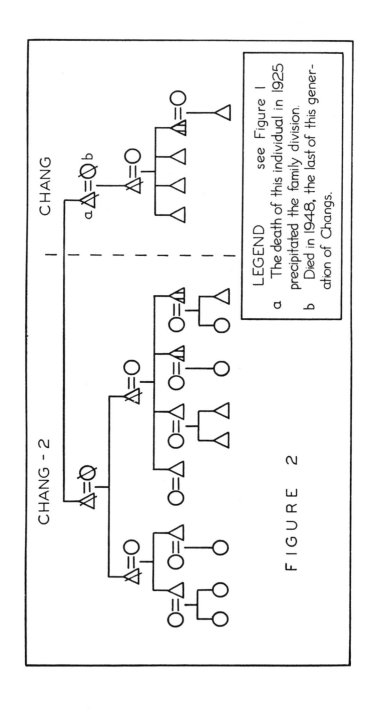

CHANG-2

CHANG

FIGURE 2

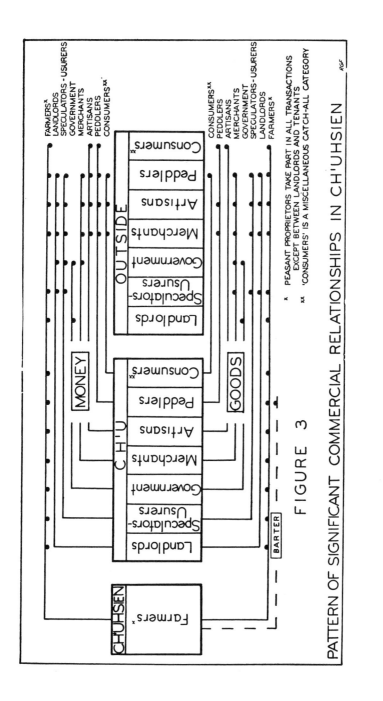

FIGURE 3

PATTERN OF SIGNIFICANT COMMERCIAL RELATIONSHIPS IN CH'UHSIEN